Genghis Khan The Emperor Of All Men

GENGHIS KHAN.

Reproduced from a painting in the possession of Kung-sing no-erh-pu
Prince of Ka-la-ch'in, a descendant of Genghis Khan.

GENGHIS KHAN
The Emperor of All Men

BY

HAROLD LAMB

LONDON

Thornton Butterworth, Ltd.

First Published	-	-	-	-	-	March, 1928
Second Impression	-		-	-	-	May, 1928
Third Impression	-		-	-	-	May, 1929
Fourth Impression	-		-	-	-	March, 1931
First Impression in the Keystone						
Library	-	-	-	-	-	November, 1933
Second Impression	-		-	-	-	March, 1934
Third Impression	-		-	-	-	May, 1936

" SCRIPTUM EST DE SAPIENTE ; IN TERRAM
ALIENARUM GENTIUM TRANSIBIT, BONA ET
MALA IN OMNIBUS TENTABIT. HIC OPUS FECIT :
SED UTINAM UT SAPIENS ET NON STULTUS.
MULTI ENIM FACIUNT QUOD FACIT SAPIENS,
SED NON SAPIENTER, SED MAGIS STULTE."

" God in Heaven. The Kha Khan, the Power of God, on Earth. The seal of the Emperor of Mankind."

THE SEAL OF GENGHIS KHAN

CONTENTS

Foreword

Part I

Part II

Part III

CONTENTS

ILLUSTRATIONS

GENGHIS KHAN

FOREWORD

THE MYSTERY

SEVEN hundred years ago a man almost conquered the earth. He made himself master of half the known world, and inspired mankind with a fear that lasted for generations.

In the course of his life he was given many names—the Mighty Manslayer, the Scourge of God, the Perfect Warrior, and the Master of Thrones and Crowns. He is better known to us as Genghis Khan.

Unlike most rulers of men, he deserved all his titles. We moderns have been taught the muster-roll of the great that begins with Alexander of Macedon, continues through the Cæsars, and ends with Napoleon. Genghis Khan was a conqueror of more gigantic stature than the well-known actors of the European stage.

Indeed it is difficult to measure him by ordinary standards. When he marched with his horde, it was over degrees of latitude and longitude instead of miles ; cities in his path were often obliterated, and rivers diverted from their courses ; deserts were peopled with the fleeing and dying, and when he had

appear to be the most brilliant of Europeans. But we cannot forget that he abandoned one army to its fate in Egypt, and left the remnant of another in the snows of Russia, and finally strutted into the *débâcle* of Waterloo. His empire fell about his ears, his Code was torn up and his son disinherited before his death. The whole celebrated affair smacks of the theatre and Napoleon himself of the play-actor.

Of necessity we must turn to Alexander of Macedon, that reckless and victorious youth, to find a conquering genius the equal of Genghis Khan—Alexander the god-like, marching with his phalanx toward the rising sun, bearing with him the blessing of Greek culture. Both died in the full tide of victory, and their names survive in the legends of Asia to-day.

Only after death the measure of their achievements differs beyond comparison. Alexander's generals were soon fighting among themselves for the kingdoms from which his son was forced to flee.

So utterly had Genghis Khan made himself master from Armenia to Korea, from Tibet to the Volga, that his son entered upon his heritage without protest, and his grandson Kubilai Khan still ruled half the world.

This empire, conjured up out of nothing by a barbarian, has mystified historians. The most recent general history of his era compiled by learned persons in England admits that it is an inexplicable fact. A worthy savant pauses to wonder at " the fateful personality of Genghis Khan, which, at bottom, we can no more account for than the genius of Shakespeare."

Many things have contributed to keep the personality of Genghis Khan hidden from us. For one thing the Mongols could not write, or did not care to do so. In consequence the annals of his day exist only in the scattered writings of the Ugurs, the Chinese, the Persians and Armenians. Not until recently was the saga of the Mongol Ssanang Setzen satisfactorily translated.

So the most intelligent chroniclers of the great Mongol were his enemies—a fact that must not be forgotten in judging him. They were men of an alien race. Moreover, like the Europeans of the thirteenth century, their conception of the world as it existed outside their own land was very hazy.

They beheld the Mongol, emerging unheralded out of obscurity. They felt the terrible impact of the Mongol horde, and watched it pass over them to other lands, unknown to them. One Mohammedan summed up sadly in these words his experience with the Mongols, "*They came, they mined, they slew—trussed up their loot and departed.*"

The difficulty of reading and comparing these various sources has been great. Not unnaturally, the orientalists who have succeeded in doing so have contented themselves mainly with the political details of the Mongol conquests. They present Genghis Khan to us as a kind of incarnation of barbaric power —a scourge that comes every so often out of the desert to destroy decadent civilizations.

The saga of Ssanang Setzen does not help to explain the mystery. It says, quite simply, that Genghis Khan was a *bogdo* of the race of gods. Instead of a mystery, we have a miracle.

The medieval chronicles of Europe incline, as we

have seen, toward a belief in a sort of Satanic power invested in the Mongol and let loose on Europe.

All this is rather exasperating—that modern historians should re-echo the superstitions of the thirteenth century, especially of a thirteenth-century Europe that beheld the nomads of Genghis Khan only as shadowy invaders.

There is a simple way of getting light on the mystery that surrounds Genghis Khan. This way is to turn back the hands of the clock seven hundred years and look at Genghis Khan as he is revealed in the chronicles of his day; not at the miracle, or the incarnation of barbaric power, but at the man himself.

We will not concern ourselves with the political achievements of the Mongols as a race, but with the man who raised the Mongols from an unknown tribe to world mastery.

To visualize this man, we must actually approach him, among his people and on the surface of the earth as it existed seven hundred years ago. We cannot measure him by the standards of modern civilization. We must view him in the aspects of a barren world peopled by hunters, horse-riding and reindeer-driving nomads.

Here, men clothe themselves in the skins of animals, and nourish themselves on milk and flesh. They grease their bodies to keep out cold and moisture. It is even odds whether they starve or freeze to death, or are cut down by the weapons of other men.

" Here are no towns or cities," says valiant Fra Carpini, the first European to enter this land, " but everywhere sandy barrens, not a hundredth part of the whole being fertile except where it is watered by rivers, which are very rare.

" This land is nearly destitute of trees, although well adapted for the pasturage of cattle. Even the emperor and princes and all others warm themselves and cook their victuals with fires of horse and cow dung.

" The climate is very intemperate, as in the middle of summer there are terrible storms of thunder and lightning by which many people are killed, and even then there are great falls of snow and such tempests of cold winds blow that sometimes people can hardly sit on horseback. In one of these we had to throw ourselves down on the ground and could not see through the prodigious dust. There are often showers of hail, and sudden, intolerable heats followed by extreme cold " :

This is the Gobi desert, A.D. 1162, the Year of the Swine in the Calendar of the Twelve Beasts.

Part I

CHAPTER I

L IFE did not matter very much in the Gobi.
Lofty plateaus, wind-swept, lying close to the
clouds. Reed bordered lakes, visited by migratory
winged creatures on their way to the northern tundras.
Huge Lake Baïkul visited by all the demons of the
upper air. In the clear nights of mid-winter, the flare
of the northern lights rising and falling above the
horizon.

Children of this corner of the northern Gobi were
not hardened to suffering ; they were born to it.
After they were weaned from their mother's milk to
mare's milk they were expected to manage for
themselves.

The places nearest the fire in the family tent
belonged to the grown warriors and to guests. Women,
it is true, could sit on the left side, but at a distance,
and the boys and girls had to fit in where they could.

So with food. In the spring when horses and cows
began to give milk in quantity, all was very well.
The sheep grew fatter, too. Game was more abundant
and the hunters of the tribe would bring in deer and
even a bear, instead of the lean fur-bearing animals
like the fox, marten and sable. Everything went into

the pot and was eaten—the able-bodied men taking the first portions, the aged and the women received the pot next, and the children had to fight for bones and sinewy bits. Very little was left for the dogs.

In the winter when the cattle were lean the children did not fare so well. Milk existed then only in the form of *kumiss*—milk placed in leather sacks and fermented and beaten. It was nourishing and slightly intoxicating for a young man of three or four years —if he could contrive to beg or steal some. Meat failing, boiled millet served to take the edge off hunger after a fashion.

The end of winter was the worst of all for the youngsters. No more cattle could be killed off without thinning the herds too much. At such a time the warriors of the tribe were usually raiding the food reserves of another tribe, carrying off cattle and horses.

The children learned to organize hunts of their own, stalking dogs and rats with clubs or blunt arrows. They learned to ride, too, on sheep, clinging to the wool.

Endurance was the first heritage of Genghis Khan, whose birth name was Temujin.[*] At the time of his birth his father had been absent on a raid against a tribal enemy, Temujin by name. The affair went well both home and afield; the enemy was made prisoner, and the father, returning, gave to his infant son the name of the captive foe.

His home was a tent made of felt stretched over a framework of wattled rods with an aperture at the

[*] Temujin signifies " The Finest Steel "—*Tumur-ji*. The Chinese version is *T'ie mou jen*, which has another meaning altogether, " Supreme Earth Man."

top to let out the smoke. This was coated with white lime and ornamented with pictures. A peculiar kind of tent, this *yurt* that wandered all over the prairies mounted on a cart drawn by a dozen or more oxen. Serviceable, too, because its dome-like shape enabled it to stand the buffeting of the wind, and it could be taken down at need.

The married women of the chieftains—and Temujin's father was a chieftain—all had their own ornamented *yurts* in which their children lived. It was the duty of the girls to attend to the *yurt*, to keep the fire burning on the stone hearth under the opening that let the smoke out. One of Temujin's sisters, standing on the platform of the cart before the entrance flap, would manage the oxen when they were on the move. The shaft of one cart would be tied to the axle of another and would creak and roll in this fashion over the level grassland where, more often than not, no single tree or bit of rising ground was to be seen.

In the *yurt* were kept the family treasures, carpets from Bokhara or Kabul, looted probably from some caravan—chests filled with women's gear, silk garments bartered from a shrewd Arab trader, and inlaid silver. More important were the weapons that hung on the walls, short Turkish scimitars, spears, ivory or bamboo bow cases—arrows of different lengths and weights, and perhaps a round shield of tanned leather, lacquered over.

These, too, were looted or purchased, passing from hand to hand with the fortunes of war.

Temujin—the youthful Genghis Khan—had many duties. The boys of the family must fish the streams

they passed in their trek from the summer to winter
pastures. The horse herds were in their charge, and
they had to ride afield after lost animals, and to search
for new pasture lands. They watched the skyline for
raiders, and spent many a night in the snow without
a fire. Of necessity, they learned to keep the saddle
for several days at a time, and to go without cooked
food for three or four days—sometimes without any
food at all.

When mutton or horse-flesh was plentiful they
feasted and made up for lost time, stowing away
incredible amounts against the day of privation.
For diversions they had horse races, twenty miles
out into the prairie and back, or wrestling matches
in which bones were freely broken.

Temujin was marked by great physical strength,
and ability to scheme—which is only another way of
adapting oneself to circumstances. He became the
leader of the wrestlers, although he was spare in
build. He could handle a bow remarkably well;
not so well as his brother Kassar who was called the
Bowman, but Kassar was afraid of Temujin.

They formed an alliance of two against their
hardy half-brothers, and the first incident related of
Temujin is the slaying of one of the half-brothers,
who had stolen a fish from him. Mercy seemed to
these nomad youths to be of little value, but retribu-
tion was an obligation.

And Temujin became aware of feuds more important than the animosity of boys. His mother, Houlun,
was beautiful, and so had been carried off by his
father from a neighbouring tribe on her wedding
ride to the tent of her betrothed husband. Houlun,

being both sagacious and wilful, made the best of circumstances after a little wailing ; but all in the *yurt* knew that some day men from her tribe would come to avenge the wrong.

At night by the glowing dung fire Temujin would listen to the tales of the minstrels, old men who rode from one wagon-tent to another carrying a one-stringed fiddle, and singing in a droning voice the tales of a tribe's forebears and heroes.

He was conscious of his strength, and his right of leadership. Was he not the first-born of Yesukai the Valiant, Khan of the Yakka or Great Mongols, master of forty thousand tents ?

From the tales of the minstrels he knew that he came of distinguished stock, the Bourchikoun, or Grey-eyed Men. He harkened to the story of his ancestor, Kabul Khan, who had pulled the emperor of Cathay by the beard and who had been poisoned as a consequence. He learned that his father's sworn brother was Toghrul Khan of the Karaïts, the most powerful of the Gobi nomads—he who gave birth in Europe to the tales of Prester John of Asia.[*]

But at that time Temujin's horizon was limited by the pasture lands of his tribe, the Yakka Mongols.

"We are not a hundredth part of Cathay," a wise counsellor said to the boy, "and the only reason why we have been able to cope with her is that we are all nomads, carrying our supplies with us, and experienced in our kind of warfare. When we can, we plunder ; when we cannot, we hide away. If we begin to build

---

[*] This name originated in Europe. At that time there were many tales of a Christian emperor who ruled inner Asia, who was known as Prester John or Presbyter Johannes. Marco Polo and others after him have chosen to identify Toghrul with the mythical Prester John.

towns and change our old habits, we shall not prosper. Besides, monasteries and temples breed mildness of character, and it is only the fierce and warlike who dominate mankind."*

When he had served his apprenticeship as herd boy, he was allowed to ride with Yesukai. By all accounts the young Temujin was good to look upon, but remarkable more for the strength of his body and a downright manner than for any beauty of features.

He must have been tall, with high shoulders, his skin a whitish tan. His eyes, set far apart under a sloping forehead, did not slant. And his eyes were green, or blue-grey in the iris, with black pupils. Long reddish-brown hair fell in braids to his back. He spoke very little, and then only after meditating on what he would say. He had an ungovernable temper and the gift of winning fast friends.

His wooing was as sudden as his sire's. While father and son were passing the night in the tent of a strange warrior, the boy's attention was attracted by the girl of the tent. He asked Yesukai at once if he could have her for a wife.

"She is young," the father objected.

"When she is older," Temujin pointed out, "she will do well enough."

Yesukai considered the girl, who was nine years of age, and ·a beauty, by name Bourtai—a name that harked back to the legendary ancestor of the tribe— the Grey-eyed.

"She is small," her father observed, secretly

* It must be remembered that the Mongols were not of the same race as the Chinese proper. They were descended from the Tungusi or aboriginal stock, with a strong mixture of Iranian and Turkish blood --a race that is now called Ural-Altaic. These were the nomads of high Asia that the Greeks named Scythians

delighted by the interest the Mongols showed, "but still, you might look at her." And of Temujin he approved. "Thy son has a clear face and bright eyes."

So the next day the bargain was struck and the Mongol Khan rode off, leaving Temujin to make the acquaintance of his future bride and father-in-law.

A few days later a Mongol galloped up with word that Yesukai, who had passed a night in the tent of some enemies and had presumably been poisoned, lay dying and had asked for Temujin. Although the thirteen-year-old boy rode as fast as a horse could carry him to the *ordu* or tent village of the clan, he found his father dead.

More than that had happened in his absence. The leading spirits of the clan had discussed matters and two thirds of them had abandoned the standard of the chieftain and had started off to find other protectors. They were afraid to trust themselves and their families and herds to an inexperienced boy.

"The deep water is gone," they said, "the strong stone is broken. What have we to do with a woman and her children?"

Houlun, the wise and courageous, did what she could to avert the break-up of the clan. Taking the standard of the nine yak-tails in her hand she rode after the deserters and pleaded with them, persuading some few families to turn back their herds and carts.

Temujin was now seated on the white horseskin, Khan of the Yakka Mongols, but he had no more than the remnant of a clan around him, and he was faced with the certainty that all the feudal foes of the Mongols would take advantage of the death of Yesukai to avenge themselves upon his son.

CHAPTER II

IN the time of his great-grandfather Kabul Khan and of his father Yesukai, the Yakka Mongols had enjoyed a kind of over-lordship in the northern Gobi. Being Mongols, as a natural consequence they had taken to themselves the best of the grazing lands that stretched from Lake Baïkul eastward to the range of mountains known now as the Khingan, on the border of modern Manchuria.

These grazing lands were very desirable, being north of the encroaching sands of the Gobi, between the two fertile valleys of the small rivers Kerulon and Onon. The hills were covered with birch and fir, and game was plentiful, water abundant—due to the late melting of the snows—circumstances only too well known to the clans that had formerly been under the dominion of the Mongol and were now preparing to seize the possessions of the thirteen-year-old Temujin.

These possessions were of inestimable value to the nomads—fertile grassland, not too bitter cold in the winter, and the herds from which they drew the necessities of life, hair to make felt and ropes to bind the *yurts*, bone for arrow tips, leather for saddles and *kumiss* sacks and harness.

Temujin, it seems, might have fled. He could do nothing to avert the coming blow. His vassals, as we may call them, were irresolute and not over-willing to pay the Khan's tithe of cattle to a boy. Besides, they were strung out through all the hills, guarding their own herds against wolves and the inevitable small raiders of early spring-time.

He did not flee. The chronicle relates that he wept for a while, solitary in the *yurt*. Then he set about the task of leadership. There were his younger brothers to feed, and his sisters and his remaining half-brother, who appears to have been devoted to the youngster. Above all, his mother, who knew only too well the inevitable disaster that must overtake her first-born.

Inevitable, because a certain warrior, Targoutai, likewise descended from the Bourchikoun, the Grey-eyed Men, had announced that he was now over-lord of the northern Gobi. Targoutai, chieftain of the Taidjuts, the feudal foes of the Mongols.

And Targoutai—who had persuaded most of Temujin's clansmen to join his standard—must now hunt down the youthful khan of the Mongols, as an older wolf seeks and slays a cub too prone to take the leadership of the pack.

The hunt was launched without warning. Throngs of horsemen galloped up to the Mongol *ordu*, the tent village, some turning aside to drive off the out-lying herds. Targoutai himself made for the tent where the standard stood.

And Temujin with his brothers fled before the onset of the warriors, Kassar, the sturdy bowman, reining in his pony to send a few arrows at his foes.

Houlun was suffered to live—Targoutai seeking no one but Temujin.

Thus the hunt began, with the Taidjuts close upon the heels of the boys. The hunters made no great haste. The trail was fresh and clear, and these nomads were accustomed to track down a horse for days if need be. So long as Temujin did not get a fresh mount, they would close in on him.

The boys headed instinctively for the shelter of gorges, with timber growth to screen them. At times they dismounted to hack down trees over the narrow track and hinder the pursuers. When twilight came upon them they separated, the younger brothers and the girls hiding in a cave, Kassar turning off, and Temujin himself riding on toward a mountain that offered concealment.

Here he kept away from the pursuers for days, until hunger made him risk an attempt to lead his horse through the waiting Taidjuts. He was seen, overtaken and brought before Targoutai who commanded that a *kang* be put upon him—a wooden yoke resting on the shoulders and holding the wrists of a captive prisoned at both ends. Thus fettered, Temujin was led off, the warriors moving back to their own grazing land, driving the captured cattle. And so he remained, helpless, until he was left with a single guard while the warriors went off to feast elsewhere. Darkness settled down on the camp, and the young Mongol was in no mood to lose an opportunity to escape.

In the murk of the tent, he struck the head of his guard with the end of the *kang*, knocking the man senseless. Running from the tent he found the moon risen and a half light through the forest in which the camp had been pitched. Plunging into the brush he made his way toward a river they had crossed the day before. And hearing the sound of pursuit behind him, he entered the water, sinking down among the rushes near the bank until only his head was above the water.

So situated, he watched the Taidjut riders search the bank for him, and he noticed that one warrior saw him, hesitated and went on without betraying him.

In the *kang* Temujin was almost as helpless as before, and it took both intuition and daring to do what he next did. He left the river, following the horsemen back into the camp, and crept to the *yurt* of the warrior who had noticed him among the rushes and had not given him away—a stranger, as it happened, stopping for the nonce with the hunters of this other clan.

At the apparition of the dripping boy the man was more frightened than Temujin. He pitied the captive, and must have reflected that the best thing to do was to rid himself of the youth. So he split the *kang* and burned up the fragments, hiding Temujin meanwhile in a cart loaded with wool.

It was hot in the loose wool—no pleasant abiding place, especially when the Taidjut warriors came to search the tent, and thrust spears into the cart, one of the blades wounding Temujin in the leg.

" The smoke of my house would have vanished, and my fire would have died out for ever had they found thee," the man remarked grimly to the fugitive, giving him at the same time food and milk and a bow with two arrows. "Go now to thy brothers and mother."

And Temujin, riding a borrowed horse, found his estate little better than that pictured by the stranger —the site of his camp filled with the ashes of fires, his herds gone, his mother and brothers vanished. He tracked them down, and discovered a hungry family in hiding, the stern Houlun, the doughty Kassar, and Belgutai the half-brother who idolized him.

They lived after a fashion, travelling by night to the camp of a distant well-wisher, with no more than eight horses in their string, trapping the more miserable game such as marmots and contenting themselves with fish instead of mutton. Temujin learned how to keep out of an ambush, and to break through the lines of men that hunted him down. Hunted he was, and his cunning grew with the years. He was not, apparently, caught a second time.

He might, even then, have fled from his ancestral grazing lands. But the youthful khan had no intention of leaving his heritage to his enemies. He visited the scattered settlements of his clan, demanding gravely the khan's tithe of the four beasts—a camel, ox, horse and sheep —to provide for his mother.

It is noticeable that he refrained from doing two things. Bourtai the Grey-eyed still awaited his coming, to bear her off to his tent, and the father of Bourtai was a powerful clansman, a leader of many spears. But Temujin did not go near them.

Nor did he appeal to the aged and influential Toghrul, the "Provider" chieftain of the Karaīt Turks, who had drunk the oath of comradeship with

Yesukai—a bond that entitled the son of one to go at
need and claim the other for foster-father. A simple
matter, perhaps, to ride over the prairies to the
Karaïts who lived in walled cities and were possessed
of real treasures, precious stones, woven stuffs, fine
weapons and even tents of cloth-of-gold—to the
Karaïts who were the people of this Prester John of
Asia.

"To go as a beggar with empty hands," Temujin
argued, "is to arouse scorn, not fellowship."

And he stuck to this determination, which was not
a matter of false pride, but a Yakka Mongol's downright way of thinking. Prester John was obliged
to aid him—an oath of comradeship is more binding
in high Asia than the pledge of a king—but he would
not make use of this master of cities and strange
wonders until he could appear before him as an
ally, not as a fugitive.

Meanwhile his eight horses were stolen.

The affair of the eight horses is worth relating in
full from the chronicle. Prowling Taidjuts were the
thieves, and Belgutai was absent at the time on the
ninth horse, a certain sorrel mare, the same that had
carried Temujin out of the clutches of Targoutai.
Belgutai was hunting marmots and when he rode in
the young khan went to his side.

"The horses have been stolen."

This was a serious matter, as it put all the brothers
but one afoot, at the mercy of any raiders who might
come along.

Belgutai offered to go for them.

"Couldst not follow and find them," objected
Kassar. "I will go."

"Ye could not find them," said Temujin, "and if ye found them ye could not bring them back. I will go."

And go he did, on the tired sorrel mare, picking up the trail of the riders and the eight horses, and following for three days. He had carried with him some dried meat, placed between the saddle and the horse's back, to soften it and keep it warm. This had given out long since, but a greater handicap was the lagging horse. The Taidjuts, being able to change from one animal to another, had kept beyond his sight.

After the fourth sunrise the young Mongol encountered a warrior of his own age milking a mare beside the trail.

"Hast thou seen eight horses and some men driving them?" Temujin asked, reining in.

"Yea, before dawn eight driven horses went past me. I will show thee the trail they took."

After a second glance at the Mongol, the strange youth hid his leather sack in some tall grass after tying it up. "Thou art tired and anxious," said he. "My name is Borchu and I will ride with thee after the horses."

The tired sorrel was turned out to graze and Borchu roped and saddled a white horse from the herd he was tending, offering it to Temujin. They took up the trail again, and came three days later within sight of the Taidjuts' camp, with the stolen horses grazing near by.

These the two youths drove off, and were promptly followed by the warriors, one of whom, mounted on a white stallion and armed with a lariat, began to overtake them.

Borchu offered to take Temujin's bow and hang back to meet the pursuers, but Temujin would have none of this. They drove on the horses until daylight began to fail, and the warrior on the white stallion was almost near enough to use his rope.

"These men might wound thee," the young Mongol said to his new comrade, " and I will use the bow."

Dropping behind, he fitted an arrow to the string and loosed it at the Taidjut who fell from the saddle, and the others drew rein when they came up with him. The two youths hurried on through the night and came in safety to the camp of Borchu's father, with the horses and the story of their exploit— Borchu hastening to find and fetch in the sack of milk to temper his father's anger.

"When I saw him weary and anxious," he explained, " I went with him."

The father, master of a large herd, listened with some satisfaction—for the tales of Temujin's adventures had passed from tent to tent over the prairies. " Ye are young," said he, " be ye friends and be ye faithful."

They gave the young khan food, filled a bag with mare's milk and sent him on his way—Borchu following not long after, with a gift of black fur for the family and the chieftain he had taken to himself.

"Without thee," Temujin greeted him, " I could not have found and brought back these horses, so half of the eight are thine."

But to this Borchu would not agree. " If I should take what is thine from thee, how couldst thou call me comrade ? "

Neither Temujin nor his youthful braves were niggards. Generosity was deep seated in him, and his memory for those who served him unfailing. As for those who warred against him—everyone outside his little band was a potential enemy.

"As a merchant trusts in his stuffs for profit," he assured his comrades, "the Mongol puts his only hope of fortune in his bravery."

In him were revealed the virtues and cruelties of that other nomad race, the Arabs. For weak characters he had little use, and he was suspicious of everything outside his clan. He had learned to match his cunning against the deceit of his enemies, but his word, when pledged to one of his own following, was inviolate.

"Word breaking," he said in after years, "is hideous in a ruler."

Even in his clan, which was now increasing by the return of warriors who had followed his father, his leadership rested on nothing more substantial than his own skill in evading his enemies and holding by hook or by crook the all-important pasture lands for his followers. Their herds and weapons, by tribal custom, belonged to themselves, not to the khan. The son of Yesukai might claim their allegiance only so long as he could protect them. Tradition—the law of the tribes—permitted the men of the clan to select another leader if Temujin should prove lacking in the ceaseless and merciless warfare of the nomad lands.

Cunning kept Temujin alive, and a growing wisdom kept the nucleus of a clan about him. Physical prowess he had, and watchfulness. The chieftains who raided the fertile region between the Kerulon and Onon could drive him from the hills into the lower plain but could not bring him to bay.

"Temujin and his brothers," it was said, "are growing in strength."

Only in Temujin did a spark of unquenchable purpose glow. He *would* be master of his heritage. At this time, when he was seventeen, he went to look for Bourtai, to carry off his first wife.

CHAPTER III

AMONG the bow-and-arrow people, the deni-
zens of the land of long days and of the high,
white mountains—as the ancient Chinese were wont
to describe the northern barbarians—there existed an
inclination to good humour, an impulse of laughter.
Because life was a thing of such incessant toil, and
the elements unfriendly, and suffering a constant
condition, any alleviation of hardships gave occasion
for merry-making. One cannot contemplate Temujin
and his Mongols without realizing that they relished
a joke ; their good humour was sometimes as overbearing as their cruelty. Their feasts were gargantuan
affairs.

Marriage and burial offered a rare occasion for
ikhüdür, for festival. Such a relaxation of the wolf-
like antagonism was Temujin's arrival at the tent
village of the father of Bourtai—several hundred
youths riding up unexpectedly, fully armed and
accoutred in sheepskins, loose tanned-leather jackets
and hideously painted lacquer breast-plates, water
sacks on the cruppers of their high saddles, lances
slung across their shoulders—dusty and grimy over
the coating of grease that protected bony faces from
the cold and bite of the wind.

" When I heard of the great enmity against thee,"

the father of Bourtai greeted the young khan, " we did not look to see thee thus alive."　.

A rare scene of laughter, and impetuous good cheer. Servants scurrying about to kill and dress sheep and fat horses for the pot, the Mongol warriors— having left their weapons at the *yurt* entrances—sitting on the right hand of the elders of the tents, drinking and clapping their hands. Before every potation, a servant hastening out to pour a libation to the quarters of the four winds, and the one-stringed fiddlers striking up.

A vista of weather-stained riders out of the plains, pulling the ears of their comrades as if to stretch wider their throats for the fermented milk and rice wine to go down the easier, and dancing clumsily in their deerskin boots.

In the tent of the chieftain, on the third day, Bourtai, sitting on the left hand, arrayed in a long dress of white felt, the braids of her hair heavy with silver coins and tiny statues, her head-dress—a cone of birch bark covered with treasured silk and supported over either ear by the whorls of braided hair— becomingly silent, until the time of her taking off, when she fled through the other tents and Temujin must needs pursue her, going through the ceremony of a struggle with her sisters and handmaids, and finally bearing her off to his horse.

A brief *ikhüdür* this, of the small-nosed beauty who departed from her tent village, astride one of Temujin's ponies. She had awaited his coming four years and she was now thirteen years of age.

So she rode, bound around the waist and breast with blue girdles, her servants bearing with them a

ARCHERY PRACTICE.

This engraving, made from a contemporary Chinese print, conveys an accurate
impression of the armour and weapons used against Genghis Khan.

sable cloak to be presented to Temujin's mother.
She was now the wife of the khan, bound to care for
his *yurt*, to milk—if need be—the animals, to watch
the herds when the men were off at war, to make felt
for the tents, to sew garments with split sinews, to
make sandals and socks for the men.

Thus her duties. And indeed she was singled out
for a destiny above that of other women. History
knows her as Bourtai Fidjen, the Empress, mother of
three sons who ruled in a later day a dominion greater
than Rome's.

The sable cloak also had its destiny. Temujin now
thought the time auspicious to visit Toghrul of the
Karaïts. He took with him his young heroes and the
sable cloak for a gift.

Toghrul Khan appears to have been a man of
integrity and a lover of peace. If not a Christian
himself, his clans were made up largely of Nestorian
Christians who had received their faith from the
early apostles of Saints Andrew and Thomas. They
held the river lands where the city of Urga is now
situated. Being largely of Turkish race they were
more given to trade and its attendant luxuries than
the Mongols.

Temujin, in this first visit to the court of—as we
may call him—his foster-father, did not ask for aid
from the powerful Karaïts and it was Toghrul who
reminded him before he rode away of the tie between
them.

But before long Temujin invoked the friendship
of the old khan. The feuds of the Gobi blazed up
anew. Unexpectedly, a formidable clan came down
from the northern plain and raided the Mongol

camp. These were the Merkits or Merguen, true barbarians descended from the aboriginal stock of the tundra region—people from the "frozen white world" where men travelled in sledges drawn by dogs and reindeer.

Dour fighters by all accounts, and clansmen of the warrior from whom Houlun had been stolen by Temujin's father some eighteen years ago, most probably they had not forgotten their old grievance. They came at night, casting blazing torches into the *ordu* of the young khan.

Temujin was able to get to a horse and clear a way to safety with his arrows, but Bourtai fell to the raiders. To satisfy tribal justice they gave her to a kinsman of the man who had lost Houlun.

The northern warrior did not long enjoy the possession of the Mongol's bride. Temujin, lacking men to launch an attack upon the Merkits, went to his foster-father Toghrul and besought the aid of the Karaïts. His request was readily granted and Mongol and Karaït descended upon the village of the raiders during a moonlight night.

The scene is described in the chronicle—Temujin riding among the disordered tents, crying the name of his lost bride—Bourtai, hearing his voice, running forth to seize his rein and be recognized.

"I have found that which I sought," the young Mongol called to his companions, dismounting from his horse.

Although he could never be certain if Bourtai's first-born were his son, his devotion to her is unmistakable. He made no distinction among his sons by her. He had other children, but these were his cherished companions. Other women and their children are no more than vague names in the chronicle.

More than once Bourtai's intuition penetrated plots against his life. We discover her at dawn, kneeling beside his bed and weeping.

"If thine enemies destroy thy heroes, majestic as cedars, what will become of thy small, weak children ? "

There was no truce in the struggle of the desert clans. The Mongols were still the weakest of the nomads who ranged the barrens beyond the great wall. The protection of Toghrul made him safe for some years from the westernmost ring of tribes, but the Taidjuts and Buyar Lake Tartars* harried him on the east with all the bitterness of old enmity. Only a body of exceeding strength and a wolf's instinct for scenting out danger kept the khan alive.

Once he was left for dead in the snow, wounded by an arrow in the throat, and two comrades discovering him sucked the blood from his wound, melting snow in a pot to wash out his hurts. The devotion of these warriors was no lip service—they stole food from an enemy camp when he lay ill, and again, when a blizzard arose on the plain, held a leather cloak as a shelter over him while he slept.

While visiting the *yurt* of a khan supposedly friendly, he discovered that a pit had been dug under an innocent-seeming carpet upon which he had been invited to sit. Temujin was soon called upon to extricate his whole clan from as bad a dilemma.

* The Tatars were a separate clan. Early Europeans by mistake applied the name Tatars to the Mongols, and " Tatary " to the Empire of the Mongol Khans. The origin of the word is Chinese—*T's T'a*, or *T's tsi*, the Far People, though the Tartars on their own account may have adopted the name of an early chieftain, Tatur.

A War Chariot of the type utilized by Genghis Khan's Chinese Opponents.

The Mongols, now grown to the strength of thirteen thousand warriors, were *en route* from summer
to winter pastures. They were scattered down a long
valley, their covered wagons, the *kibitkas* or tent carts,
trundling along within the slow moving herds, when
word was brought to the khan that a horde of foemen had appeared on the sky-line and was moving
swiftly down upon him.

No heir-apparent of Europe ever faced a similar
situation.

The enemy materialized into thirty thousand
Taidjuts led by Targoutai. To flee meant the sacrifice
of women, cattle and all the clan's possessions; to
muster his fighting bands and ride out to meet the
Taidjuts would lead inevitably to his being surrounded
by greater numbers, his men cut down or scattered.

It was a crisis of nomad life in which the clan faced
destruction, and it called for instant decision and
action by the khan.

Promptly and in a fashion all his own Temujin
met the crisis. By now all his warriors were mounted
and gathering under the various standards. Drawing
them up in lines of squadrons with one flank protected
by a wood, he formed upon the other flank a large
hollow square of the *kibitkas*. The cattle he drove into
this square, and into the carts he hurried the women
and the boys who were armed with bows.

He now prepared to face the charge of the thirty
thousand who were crossing the valley. They were
in full array, drawn up in squadrons of five hundred.
These squadrons had a hundred men in a rank and
were in consequence five ranks deep.

The first two lines wore armour—heavy plates of

iron, pierced and knotted together with thongs, and helmets of iron or hard, lacquered leather surmounted with horsehair crests. The horses, too, were barded —their necks, chests and flanks covered with leather. Their riders bore small, round shields and lances with horsehair tufts beneath the points.

But these ranks of armoured riders halted while the rearmost lines passed through them—men wearing only tanned leather and armed with javelins and bows. These, on nimble horses, wheeled in front of the Mongols launching their weapons and screening the advance of the heavy cavalry.

Temujin's men, armed and equipped in like manner, met the onset with flights of arrows, driven from powerful bows strengthened with horn.

This skirmishing ceased when the Taidjut light cavalry wheeled back into position behind the armoured ranks and the massed squadrons advanced at a gallop.

Then Temujin loosed his Mongols to meet them. But he had drawn up his clans in double squadrons, in masses of a thousand, ten deep. Though he had only thirteen units and the Taidjuts sixty bands, the charge of his deeper formations along that narrow front checked the Taidjut advance and scattered the leading squadrons.

Temujin was now able to throw his heavy masses against the lighter squadrons of his foe. The Mongols, separating and whirling as they went forward following the standard of the nine yak-tails, loosed their arrows on either hand.

There ensued one of the terrible steppe struggles —mounted hordes, screaming with rage, closing in under arrow flights, wielding short sabres, pulling their foes from the saddle with thrown lariats and hooks attached to the ends of lances. Each squadron fought as a separate command, and the fighting ranged up and down the valley as the warriors scattered under a charge, reformed and came on again.

It lasted until daylight left the sky. Temujin had won a decisive victory. Five or six thousand of the enemy had fallen and seventy chiefs were led before him with swords and quivers hanging from their necks.

Some accounts have it that the Mongol khan caused the seventy to be boiled alive in cauldrons on the spot—an improbable touch of cruelty. The young khan had little mercy in him, but knew the value of able-bodied captives to serve him.[*]

* See Note I, The Massacres, page 209.

CHAPTER IV

THE red-haired khan of the Mongols had fought his first pitched battle and won it. He could now carry with pride the ivory or horn baton, shaped like a small mace, that belonged by right to a general —a leader of men.

And he was obsessed by a hunger for men to serve him. No doubt this hunger had its source in the misery of the lean years when Borchu had pitied him, and the arrows of thick-headed Kassar had saved his life.

But Temujin measured strength not in terms of political power, upon which he had pondered little as yet, or of wealth which seemed to be of scant use. Being a Mongol, he wanted only what he needed. His conception of strength was man-power. When he praised his heroes he said that they had crushed hard stones into gravel, overturned cliffs and stopped the rush of deep waters.

Above everything, he looked for loyalty. Treachery was the unpardonable sin of the clansman. A traitor might bring about the destruction of a whole tent village, or lead a horde into ambush. Loyalty to the clan—and the khan, be it said—was the *ultimum desideratum*. " What shall be said of a man who will make a promise at dawn and break it at nightfall ? "

45

An echo of his longing for men is heard in his prayer. The Mongol was accustomed to go to the summit of a bare mountain which he believed to be the abiding place of the *tengri*, the spirits of the upper air that loosed the whirlwinds and thunder and all the awe-inspiring phenomena of the boundless sky. He prayed to the quarters of the four winds, his girdle over his shoulders.

"Illimitable Heaven, do Thou favour me ; send the spirits of the upper air to befriend me ; but on earth send men to aid me."

And men flocked to the standard of the nine yak-tails in great numbers, no longer by families and tens but by hundreds. A wandering clan, at feud with its former khan, gravely discussed the merits of Temujin of the Mongols—"He permits the hunter to keep all game slain in the great hunts ; after a battle each man keeps his just share of spoil. He has taken the coat from his back and given it as a present ; he has come down from the horse he had mounted, and has given it to the needy."

No collector ever welcomed a rare acquisition as eagerly as the Mongol khan hailed these wanderers.

He was gathering about him a court, without chamberlains or councillors, made up of warlike spirits. Borchu and Kassar were there, of course— his first brothers-in-arms—and Arghun the lute player, Bayan and Muhuli—two crafty and battle-scarred generals—and Soo, the great crossbow-man.

Arghun appears to have been a genial spirit, if not a minstrel. We have one clear glimpse of him when he borrowed a favourite gold lute of the khan and lost it. The quick tempered Mongol fell into a rage and sent two of his paladins to slay Arghun. Instead of doing so they seized the offender and make him drink two skinfuls of wine. Then they hid him away. On the following day they roused him out of torpor and led him to the *yurt* entrance of the khan at daybreak, exclaiming, "The light already shines in thine *ordu*,* O Khan. Open the entrance and display thy clemency."

Seizing this moment of silence, Arghun sang :

"While the thrush sings *ting-tang*
The hawk pounces on him before the last note—
So did the wrath of my lord fall on me.
Alas, I love the flowing bowl, but am no thief !"

Though theft was punishable by death, Arghun was pardoned, and the fate of the golden lute remains a mystery to this day.

These paladins of the khan were known throughout the Gobi as the *Kiyat*, or Raging Torrents. Two of them, mere boys at this time, carried devastation over ninety degrees of longitude in a later day—Chepé Noyon, the Arrow Prince, and Subotai Bahadur, the Valiant.

Chepé Noyon appears on the scene as the youth of a hostile clan, hunted after a battle until he was surrounded by Mongols led by Temujin. He had no horse and he asked for one, offering to fight any man among the Mongols. Temujin granted his request, giving the youthful Chepé a swift white-nosed horse. When he had mounted, Chepé managed to cut his way through the Mongols and escape. Later he returned and said that he wished to serve the khan.

*Ordu, the centre of the clan, the tent village.

Long afterwards, when Chepé Noyon was ranging through the T'ian shan, hunting down Gutchluk of Black Cathay, he gathered together a drove of a thousand white-nosed horses and sent it to the khan as a gift and a token that he had not forgotten the incident that spared his life.

Less impetuous than young Chepé but more sagacious was Subotai of the Uriankhi, the reindeer people. In him existed something of Temujin's grimness of purpose. Before an engagement with the Tatars, the khan called for an officer to lead the first onset. Subotai came forward and was praised for his action and asked to select a hundred picked warriors to serve as a bodyguard.

Subotai replied that he wanted no one to accompany him. He intended to go alone, in advance of the horde.

Temujin, doubting, gave him permission to depart, and Subotai rode into the camp of the Tatars with the explanation that he had forsaken the khan and wished to join their clan. He convinced them that the Mongol horde was not in the vicinity, and they were utterly unprepared when the Mongols descended upon them and scattered them.

" I will ward off thy foes," Subotai promised the young khan, " as felt protects from the wind. That is what I will do for thee."

" When we capture beautiful women and splendid stallions," his paladins assured him, " we will bring all to thee. If we transgress thy commands or work harm to thee, leave us out in the wild barren places to perish."

" I was like a sleeping man when ye came to me,"

Temujin made answer to his heroes, " I was sitting in sadness aforetime and ye roused me."

They hailed him for what he was in reality, khan of the Yakka Mongols, and he apportioned to each of the paladins praise and honours, taking into account the character of each man.

Borchu, he said, would sit nearest him in the *kurultai*, the assemblage of the chieftains, and would be among the number that had the right of carrying the khan's bow and quiver. Others were to be masters of nourishment, having charge of the herds. Still others were masters of the *kibitkas*, and of the servants. Kassar, who possessed physical strength and not too much discrimination, he named sword-bearer.

Temujin was careful to single out discerning men as well as daring for his lieutenants—the leaders of the armed horde. He knew the value of the cunning that could bridle anger and wait for the proper moment to strike a blow. Indeed, the very essence of the Mongol character is its patience. The men who were brave and foolhardy he allowed to look after the *kibitkas*, and the all-important supplies. The stupid were left to tend herd.

Of one leader he said : " No man is more valiant than Yessoutai ; no one has rarer gifts. But, as the longest marches do not tire him, as he feels neither hunger nor thirst, he believes that his officers and soldiers do not suffer from such things. That is why he is not fitted for high command. A general should think of hunger and thirst, so he may understand the suffering of those under him, and he should husband the strength of his men and beasts."

D

To keep his authority over this court of " venomous fighters " the young khan needed all his grim determination, and a nicely balanced sense of justice. The chieftains who came to his standard were as unruly as Vikings. The chronicle relates how Bourtai's father appeared with his followers and his seven grown sons to present to the khan. Gifts were exchanged, and the seven sons took their place among the Mongols, stirring up no end of bitterness—especially one who was a *shaman*, Tebtengri by name. Being a *shaman*, he was supposed to be able to leave his body at will and enter the spirit world. His was the gift of prophecy.

And in Tebtengri there was fierce ambition. After spending some days in the different tents of the chieftains, he and some of his brothers set upon Kassar and beat him with fists and sticks.

Kassar complained to the khan, Temujin.

" Thou who hast boasted," replied his brother, " that no man is thine equal in strength or cunning —why let these fellows beat thee ? "

Vexed by this, Kassar went off to his own quarters in the *ordu* and kept away from Temujin. In this interval, Tebtengri sought out the khan. " My spirit hath listened to words in the other world," he said, " and this truth is known to me from Heaven itself. Temujin will rule his people for a while, but then Kassar will rule. If thou put not an end to Kassar thy rule will not long endure."

The cunning of the priest-conjurer had its effect on the khan, who could not forget what he took to be a prophecy. That evening he mounted his horse and went with a small following of warriors to seize

Kassar. Word of this reached Houlun, his mother.
She ordered her servants to make ready a cart drawn
by a swift-paced camel, and hastened after the khan.

She reached Kassar's tents and passed through the
warriors who had surrounded them. Entering the
chief *yurt* she found Temujin facing Kassar who was
on his knees with his cap and girdle taken from him.
The khan was angry, and the fear of death had come
to his younger brother, the Bowman.

Houlun, a woman of resolution, undid Kassar's
bonds and brought him his cap and girdle. Kneeling,
she bared her breasts, and spoke to Temujin. "Ye
two have drunk from these breasts. Temujin, thou
hast many gifts, but Kassar alone has the strength
and skill to shoot arrows without failing. When men
have rebelled against thee, he has brought them down
with his arrows."

The young khan listened in silence, waiting until
the anger of his mother had ceased. Then he left
the *yurt*, saying, "I was frightened when I acted
thus. Now I am ashamed."

Tebtengri continued to circulate through the tents
and stir up trouble. Claiming supernatural revelations
as sponsors of his plots, he was a good deal of a thorn
in the side of the Mongol khan. He gathered quite a
following, and being an ambitious soul, believed that
he could undermine the influence of the young
warrior. Fearing to come into conflict with Temujin,
he and his companions sought out Temugu, the
youngest brother of the khan, and forced him to
kneel to them.

Tradition forbade the use of weapons in deciding
quarrels among the Mongols, but after this act of the

shaman, Temujin sent for Temugu and spoke to him. "This day Tebtengri will come to my *yurt.* Deal with him as pleases thee."

His position was no easy one. Munlik, chieftain of a clan and father of Bourtai, had aided him in many a war and had been honoured accordingly. Tebtengri himself was a *shaman,* a prophet and a wizard. Temujin, the khan, was expected to play the part of judge in dealing with quarrels—not to indulge his own wishes.

He was alone in the tent, sitting by the fire when Munlik entered with his seven sons. He greeted them, and they seated themselves on his right, when Temugu entered. All weapons, of course, had been left at the *yurt* entrance, and the youngster caught Tebtengri by the shoulders. "Yesterday I was forced to kneel to thee, but to-day I will try strength with thee."

For a while they struggled and the other sons of Munlik rose to their feet.

"Wrestle not here!" Temujin called to the two adversaries. "Go outside."

By the entrance of the *yurt* three strong wrestlers were waiting—had been waiting for this moment, whether instructed by Temugu or the khan. They seized Tebtengri as he came forth, broke his spine and threw him aside. Without moving, he lay near the wheel of a cart.

"Tebtengri forced me to my knees yesterday," Temugu cried to his brother the khan. "Now, when I wish to try strength with him, he lies down and will not rise."

Munlik and his six sons went to the door, looked

SHAMAN TUBUNGRI, THE MONGOL WIZARD
From an old French Work on Tatary

out, and saw the body of the *shaman*. Then grief troubled the old chieftain and he turned to Temujin. "O Khan, I have served thee, *until this day !*"

His meaning was clear, and his six sons made ready to rush upon the Mongol. Temujin stood up. He had no weapon and there was no way out of the *yurt* except the entrance. Instead of calling for aid he spoke sternly to the angry clansmen. "Aside! I wish to go out!"

Surprised by the unexpected command, they gave way, and he went from the tent to the guard post of his warriors. So far the affair had been only an incident in the never-ending feuds around the red-headed khan. But he wished to avoid, if possible, a blood feud with Munlik's clan. A glance at the body of the *shaman* told him that Tebtengri was dead. He ordered his own *yurt* to be moved, so it covered the body, and the entrance flap was tied shut.

During the next night Temujin sent two of his men to lift the body of the priest conjurer through the smoke hole at the top of the tent. When curiosity began to be aroused among the men of the *ordu* as to the fate of the wizard, Temujin opened the entrance flap and enlightened them.

"Tebtengri made plots against my brothers and struck them, and now the spirits of Heaven have taken away both his life and his body."

But to Munlik when they were alone together again he spoke gravely. "Thou didst not teach thy sons obedience, though they had need of it. This one tried to make himself my equal, and so I put an end to him, as I have to others. As for thee, I have promised to spare thee from death in every case. So let us end this matter." *

There was no end, however, to the tribal warfare of the Gobi, to the wolf-like struggle of the great clans—the harrying and the hunting down. Though the Mongols were still one of the weaker peoples, a hundred thousand tents now followed the standard of the khan. His cunning protected them, his fierce courage emboldened his warriors. Instead of a few families, the responsibility of a people rested upon his shoulders. He himself could sleep sound of nights ; his herds, increased by the khan's tithe, grew comfortably. He was more than thirty years of age, in the fullness of his strength, and his sons now rode with him, looking about for wives, as he had once travelled the plains at Yesukai's side. He had gleaned his heritage from his enemies, and he meant to hold it.

But there was something else in his mind, a plan half formed, a wish half expressed.

" Our elders have always told us," he said one day before the council, " that different hearts and minds cannot be in one body. But this I intend to bring about. I shall extend my authority over my neighbours."

To mould the " venomous fighters " into one confederacy of clans, to make his feudal enemies his subjects. That was his thought. And he set about realizing it with all his really great patience.

---

* The Mongol saga of Ssanang Setzen is rather allegorical, and gives the impression that the events in the Gobi were caused by the prowess, the cunning or the treachery of a few men. In reality the conspiracy of the shaman lasted a long time and involved strong parties on both sides. It was as important in its way as the combat between church and king that marked the reign of Frederick II and Innocent IV in Europe not long after.

CHAPTER V

WITH the wars of the nomad clans—Tatars and Mongols, Merkits and Karaïts, Naimans and Ugurs that passed and repassed across the high prairies from the great wall of Cathay to the far mountains of mid-Asia in the west—we are not here concerned. The twelfth century was drawing to its end, and Temujin was still labouring at what his elders told him could not be brought about, a confederacy of the clans. It could only come in one way, by the supremacy of one clan over the others.

The Karaïts, in their cities on the caravan route from the northern gates of Cathay to the west, held what might be called the balance of power. To Toghrul, called Prester John, went Temujin with the suggestion of an alliance. The Mongols were strong enough now for him to do so fittingly.

"Without thy assistance, O my father, I cannot survive unmolested. Thou, too, canst not live on in peace without my firm friendship. Thy false brothers and cousins would invade thy land and divide thy pastures between them. Thy son hath not wisdom to see this at present, but he would be reft of power and life if thine enemies prevail. Our one way to keep our authority and survive is through a friendship nothing can shatter. Were I thy son also, matters would be settled for both of us."

It was Temujin's right to claim adoption by the elder khan, and Prester John gave assent. He was old, and he had a liking for the young Mongol.

To his compact Temujin remained faithful. When the Karaïts were driven out of their lands and cities by the western tribes which were largely Moham-medans and Buddhists and cherished a warm religious hatred of the Christian-shamanistic Karaïts, the Mongol sent his Raging Torrents to aid the discomfited chieftain.

And, tentatively—as the ally of the old Karaït—he essayed statecraft.

The opportunity was an excellent one, to his thinking. Behind the great wall the Golden Emperor of Cathay* stirred in his sleep and remembered inroads of the Buyar Lake Tatars that had annoyed his frontiers. He announced that he himself would lead a grand expedition beyond the wall to punish the offending tribesmen—an announcement that filled his subjects with alarm. Eventually a high officer was dispatched with a Cathayan army against the Tatars, who retired as usual unscathed and unchastened. The host of Cathay, being composed largely of foot soldiers, could not come up with the nomads.

Tidings of this reached Temujin, who acted as swiftly as hard-whipped ponies could bear his messages across the plains. He rallied all his clansmen and sent

* Thirteenth century China, which was then divided between the Chin, or Gold dynasty in the north and the older Sung dynasty in the south. Cathay itself is derived from K'itai, the Tatar word for China and the dynasty that had given way to the Chin. In middle Asia and Russia to-day China is still called K'itai. The early voyagers out of Europe brought the name back with them.

EASTERN ASIA, AT THE END OF THE TWELFTH CENTURY.

I. The Chin Empire; II. The Empire of the Lung; III. The Kingdom of
Hia; IV. The Empire of Black Cathay.

to Prester John, reminding his elder ally that the
Tatars were the clan that had slain his father. The
Karaïts answered his call, and the combined hordes
rode down upon the Tatars, who could not retreat
because the Cathayans were in their rear.

The ensuing battle broke the power of the Tatars,
added numbers of captives to the victorious clans, and
gave the officer of the expeditionary force of Cathay
an opportunity to claim all credit for himself, which
he did. He rewarded Prester John with the title of
Wang Khan, or Lord of Kings, and Temujin with the
brevet of " Commander Against Rebels "—an emolu-
ment that cost the Cathayan nothing at all, except a
silver cradle covered with cloth of gold. Both title
and gift must have astonished the hard-fighting
Mongol rarely. At any rate the cradle, the first ever
seen in the barrens, was put on view in the tent of
the khan.

New warriors joined the ranks of the Raging
Torrents. Temujin could watch his sons go forth
with Chepé Noyon, the Arrow Lord, who had a
weakness for wearing sable boots and silvered mail
that he had plundered from a wandering Cathayan.
Chepé Noyon was never satisfied unless he was afield
with a band of partisans to gallop after him. A good
tutor for the eldest son Juchi—the Guest—born under
a shadow, moody and defiant, and yet bold enough
in spirit to delight the khan.

It was the last of the twelfth century ; Temujin
had led his household people on a hunt down the
rivers toward the Karaït land, flinging wide the circle
of riders. They had driven a good number of antelope,

THE KHARESMIAN EMPIRE AT THE BEGINNING OF THE THIRTEENTH CENTURY,
SHOWING THE POSITION OF THE OTHER MOHAMMEDAN POWERS.

some deer and lesser game, and closed the circle,
making play with stout curved bows until the last
living creature lay among the boulders.   No dallying
about a Mongol hunt.

The covered *kibitkas* and the camel carts awaited
them, off somewhere in the prairie, and the hunters
returning, the oxen were unspanned.   The wattles
of the *yurts* were set up and the felt covering drawn
taut over the framework.   Fires lighted.

Much of the game was to be kept as a gift for old
Toghrul, now Wang Khan.   The Karaïts had been
overbearing to the Mongols.   Spoil, rightly belonging
to Temujin's men, had been taken by the men of
Wang Khan, and the Mongol had suffered this.

He had too many enemies in the lands of the
Karaïts, descendants of the Bourchikoun who wished
to oust him from the khanship and the favour of the
Karaït lord.   So he was going to his foster-father.
It had been agreed between them that if any differ-
ence arose, one would not act against the other, but
that they would meet together and talk quietly until
the truth of the matter was clear to them.

Temujin had learned much from bitter experience.
On the death of Wang Khan he knew there would be
war anew ; but among the Karaïts were groups of
warriors who favoured him.   The bodyguard of Wang
Khan, urged by the enemies of the Mongol khan to
seize him, had refused.   And offers of marriage had
been sent to the Mongols.   The Karaïts had a bride
for Juchi among the girls of the chieftain's family.

But Temujin remained in his camp, keeping his
distance warily from the Karaït *ordus*, while his men
went before him to see if the way were safe.   His

riders did not return, but two horse-herds galloped in at night with news of the Karaïts, news both unwelcome and ominous.

His enemies in the west—Chamuka the Cunning, Toukta Beg, chieftain of the dour Merkits, the son of Wang Khan, and Temujin's uncles—had determined to put an end to him. They had chosen Chamuka as *gurkhan*. They had persuaded the ageing and hesitant Wang Khan to throw his strength in with theirs. The marriage overtures had been a ruse—as Temujin half suspected.

His efforts at statecraft had failed. He had been working, it seems, to keep the Karaïts at war with the western Turkish tribes while he strengthened himself in the east ; and to keep Wang Khan allied to him until his eastern clans were strong enough to face the Karaïts on an equal footing. His policy had been judicious, but his guile had been met by greater cunning, and now by treachery.

The Karaïts—so the two herdsmen told him—were drawing near his camp, intending to rush upon it during the night and slay him in his tent with arrows.

The situation was nearly desperate, since the Karaïts would be in greater force, and Temujin had the families of his warriors to preserve if possible. Of armed men he had six thousand—some accounts place the number at less than three thousand. He had been warned and he lost not a minute in acting.

He sent the guards of his own *yurt* through the encampment, rousing the sleepers, warning the leaders, and routing out the herd boys. The herds were driven off, to be stampeded before daylight and scattered as much as possible. No way to save them, more than

that. The people of the *ordu* hastened to mount the
horses that were always kept at hand, and to fill the
lighter camel carts with their chests and women.
Without wailing or any argument began the long trek
back to their encampments.

The *yurts* and the great ox-carts he left standing as
they were, and detached a few men with good horses
to keep the fires burning high. With his officers and
the best of his clansmen he retired slowly, covering
the retreat. No chance, now, to escape the storm that
was drawing near under the screen of darkness.

They rode eight or nine miles toward a mass of
hills that would offer some shelter to his men if they
were forced to scatter. After crossing a stream, he
halted his riders within a gorge, before the horses
should become weary.

Meanwhile the Karaïts had swept into his deserted
camp before daybreak and had pierced through with
their arrows the white felt tent of the khan before they
noticed the silence of the place, the absence of the
herds and the standard. They had then an interval
of confusion and consultation. The bright fires had
led them to think the Mongols were still within the
yurts. And when they understood the tents had been
left, with carpets and utensils—even the spare saddles
and milk sacks—it seemed to them that the Mongols
had fled from them in fear and without order.

The broad trail to the east could not be hidden by
darkness, and the clans of the Karaïts took up the
pursuit at once. They went at a gallop, and they
arrived at the foothills after dawn, with the dust
clouds rolling up behind them. Temujin watched
their approach, and saw that they had stretched out

in the swift ride. The clans were scattered, the best horses forging ahead of the slower-paced.

Instead of waiting longer in the gorge he led out his warriors in close array, their horses rested. They crossed the stream and scattered the vanguard of the Karaïts, and formed across the rolling grassland, covering the retreat of the *ordu*. Then Wang Khan and his chieftains came up. The Karaïts were re-alined, and the desperate battle of extermination began.

Temujin had never been harder pressed. He had need then of all the personal valour of his Raging Torrents, and the steadiness of his household clans, the heavily armed riders of the Urut and Manhut clans that had always served him. His numbers did not allow him to make a frontal attack and he was reduced to holding what little advantage the ground gave him—which meant a last resort with Mongols. As the day drew to its close, with inevitable defeat in store for him, he called upon one of his sworn brothers, Guïldar the standard keeper, chieftain of the Manhuts, and ordered him to circle the array of the Karaïts and take and keep a hill on their left rear, a hill known as Gupta.

"O Khan, my brother," responded the weary Guïldar, "I will mount my best horse and break through all who oppose me. I will plant thy yak-tailed standard on Gupta. I will show thee my valour, and if I fall, do thou nourish and rear my children. It is all one to me when my end comes."

This circling movement was the favourite man-œuvre of the Mongols, the *tulughma*, or "standard sweep" that turns an enemy's flank and takes him in the rear. With his clans scattered and the Karaïts breaking through his lines, and darkness coming on, it was now no more than a desperate effort of defiance ; but the stalwart Guïldar did reach the hill and plant his standard, and hold his ground. It held the Karaïts in restraint, especially as the son of Wang Khan had been wounded in the face with an arrow.

When the sun set, the Karaïts and not the Mongols, withdrew a little from the field. Temujin waited only to cover Guïldar's withdrawal, and to gather up the wounded paladins—two of his sons among them—who rode in on captured horses, sometimes two men on a single animal. Then he fled to the east, and the Karaïts took up the pursuit the next day.

It had been the most desperate of Temujin's battles, and he had been defeated. But he had kept the nucleus of his clansmen intact, himself alive and the *ordu* safeguarded.

"We have fought," said Wang Khan, "a man with whom we should never have quarrelled."

In Mongol legend it is still repeated how Guïldar bore the standard to Gupta.

But on the long retreat, such was the necessity of life in the barrens, the warriors "licking their wounds" on their spent horses flung out again the circle of hunters to gather in antelope and deer—whatever they could reach with their arrows. No love of sport impelled them to do this. Food must be gleaned for the *ordu*.

CHAPTER VI

THE immediate effect of the Karaït victory was to strengthen the alliance against Temujin. Chieftains of the nomads were well inclined to ally themselves with a growing power; it meant protection and greater wealth for them.

To Wang Khan the angry Mongol sent eloquent reproach.

"O Khan, my father, when thou wert pursued by enemies, did I not send my four heroes to aid thee? Thou didst come to me on a blind horse, thy garments in tatters, thy body nourished only by the meat of a single sheep. Did I not give thee abundance of sheep and horses?

"In times gone by, thy men kept the booty of battle that was mine by right. Then it all was lost to thee, taken by thy foes. My heroes restored it. Then, by the Black River we swore we would not listen to the evil words of those who would divide us, but would meet and talk together of the matter. I have not said, 'My reward is slight, I have need of a greater.'

"When a wheel of an ox-cart breaks, the oxen cannot go forward. Am I not a wheel of thy *kibitka*? Why art thou angered because of me? Why dost thou attack me now?"

In this can be detected an echo of contempt. And the reproach is rather for the wavering man who did not know his own mind—Prester John mounted on a blind horse.

Temujin set about making the best of things with his dogged determination. Couriers were sent to the near-by clans and soon the khans of his own domain and their neighbours were kneeling on either side of the white horse skin of the Mongol chieftain, their feet tucked under them decorously, their long coats bound with ornamented girdles, their lined, bronzed faces peering through the smoke of the *yurt* fire. The council of the khans.

Each one spoke in turn, the Bourchikoun, the Grey-eyed Men, many of whom had tasted defeat at the hands of Temujin. Some wished to give in to the powerful Karaïts and submit to the overlordship of Prester John and his son. The bolder spirits raised their voices for battle, and offered to give the baton of leadership to Temujin. This counsel prevailed.

Temujin, in accepting the baton, said that his orders must be obeyed in all the clans, and he must be allowed to punish whom he saw fit. "From the beginning I have said to you that the lands between the three rivers must have a master. You would not understand. Now, when you fear that Wang Khan will treat you as he has treated me, you have chosen me for a leader. To you I have given captives, women, *yurts* and herds. Now I shall keep for you the lands and customs of our ancestors."

During that winter the Gobi became divided into two rival camps, the peoples east of Lake Baïkul arming against the western confederacy. This time

Temujin was first in the field, before snow left the valleys. With his new allies he advanced without warning on the camp of Wang Khan.

The chronicle gives an amusing insight into the trickery of the nomads. Temujin had sent a Mongol into the enemy lines to complain of ill-treatment, and to say that the Mongol horde was still far distant from the camp. The Karaïts, not too credulous, dispatched several riders on picked mounts to go back with this warrior and see for themselves the truth of the matter.

Not far from the Karaït camp, the single Mongol warrior who was keeping his eyes about him, beheld the standard bar of Temujin's clans on the other side of a knoll they were climbing. He knew that his captors were well mounted and could gallop clear if they noticed the standard. So he dismounted and busied himself about his horse. When asked what he was doing, he said :

" A stone is in one of the hoofs."

By the time the sagacious Mongol had relieved his horse of the imaginary stone, Temujin's vanguard came over the rise and made the Karaïts prisoners. Wang Khan's camp was attacked and a bitter struggle began.

By nightfall the Karaïts were broken, Wang Khan and his son both wounded and fleeing. Temujin rode into the captured camp, and gave to his men the wealth of the Karaïts, the saddles covered with coloured silk and soft, red leather, the thin and finely tempered sabres, the plates and goblets of silver. Such things could not serve him. The tent of Wang Khan, hung with cloth-of-gold, he gave entire to the two herders who had warned him of the Karaït advance that first night near Gupta.

Following up the centre of the Karaïts, he surrounded them with his warriors and offered them their lives if they would yield. " Men fighting as ye have done to save your lord, are heroes. Be ye among mine, and serve me."

The remnants of the Karaïts joined his standard, and he pushed forward to their city in the desert, Karakorum, the Black Sands.

His cousin, Chamuka the Cunning, was made captive afterward and brought before him.

" What fate dost thou expect ? " Temujin asked.

" The same that I would have bestowed upon thee, had I taken thee ! " responded Chamuka without hesitation. " The slow death."

He meant the Chinese torture of slow dismemberment that begins the first day with cutting off the joints of the little fingers and continues up all the limbs. Surely there was no lack of courage among the descendants of the Bourchikoun. Temujin, however, followed the custom of his people, which forbids shedding the blood of a chieftain of high birth, and sent away Chamuka to be strangled with a silk bowstring, or stifled between heavy felts.

Prester John, who had entered the war unwillingly, fled hopelessly beyond his lands and was put to death by two warriors of a Turkish tribe. His skull, the chronicle relates, was set in silver and remained in the tent of this chieftain, an object of veneration. His son was killed in much the same manner.*

A nomad chieftain might have been expected to content himself with the fruits of such a victory. And the results of a nomad conquest have ever been the

* See Note II, Prester John of Asia, page 212.

same—a gathering of spoil, idleness or restlessness, then quarrels or a dividing up of the haphazard empire of the wanderers.

Temujin showed himself made of different stuff. He had now a core of a kingdom in the Karaïts who had cultivated the soil and built cities—of dried mud and thatch, it is true, but still permanent abiding places. Using every effort to keep the Karaïts settled and reconciled, he launched his hordes into new conquests without a moment's delay.

" The merit of an action," he told his sons, " is in finishing it to the end."

In the three years following the battle that gave him the mastery of the Gobi, he thrust his veteran horsemen far into the valleys of the western Turks, the Naimans and Ugurs, people of a superior culture. They had been the foes of Prester John, and might have banded together to resist Temujin, but he gave them no time to realize what was in store for them. From the long white mountains of the north, down the length of the great wall, through the ancient cities of Bishbalik and Khoten his officers galloped.

Marco Polo has a word to say here, of Temujin.

" When he conquered a province he did no harm to the people or their property, but merely established some of his own men in the country among them, while he led the remainder to the conquest of other provinces. And when those whom he had conquered became aware how well and safely he protected them against all others, and how they suffered no ill at his hands, and saw what a noble prince he was, then they joined him heart and soul and became his devoted followers. And when he had thus gathered such a multitude that they seemed to cover the earth, he began to think of conquering a great part of the world."

The fate of his old enemies was hardly as desirable as this. Once he had broken the armed power of a hostile clan, the Mongol hunted down all men of the reigning family and put them to death. The fighting men of the clan were divided up among more dependable people ; the most desirable women were taken as wives by his warriors—others were made slaves. Wandering children were adopted by Mongol mothers, and the grazing lands and herds of the defeated clan turned over to new owners.

Temujin's life, up to this point, had been shaped by his enemies. From adversity he had gained strength of body and the wolflike wisdom that seemed to lead him to do instinctively the right thing. Now he was strong enough to make conquests on his own account. And after the first overthrow of the men who faced him with weapons, he proved an indulgent master.

He was entering new parts of the world, the age-old caravan routes and cities of Central Asia, and a vast curiosity stirred in him. He noticed among the captives men richly dressed and upright in bearing, who were not warriors, and he learned that they were savants—astrologers who knew the stars—physicians who understood the use of herbs such as rhubarb and the ailments of sick women.

A certain Ugur, who had served a defeated chieftain, was brought before him still holding a small gold object curiously wrought.

"Why dost thou cling to that ?" the Mongol asked.

" I wished," responded the faithful minister, " to care for it until the death of him who entrusted it to me."

" Thou art a loyal subject," the khan admitted, " but he is dead, and his land, all he possessed, is now mine. Tell me what this token is good for."

" Whenever my lord wished to levy silver or grain, he gave a commission to one of his subjects ; it was necessary to mark his orders with this seal to show that they were in reality royal commands."

Temujin promptly ordered a seal to be made for himself, and one was fashioned of green jade. He pardoned the captive Ugur, gave him a position in his court with instructions to teach his children the writing of the Ugurs, which is a form of Syriac taught, in all probability, by Nestorian priests long since dead.

But to his paladins fell the greatest reward—to those who had aided the khan in some crisis. They were created *tar-khans*, and raised above all others. They had the right of entering the royal pavilion at any time without ceremony. They could make the first selection of their share of spoil taken in any war, and were exempt from all tithes. More than that, they could do, actually, no wrong. Nine times would the death punishment be forgiven them. Whatever lands they selected, they were to have, and these privileges would be inherited by their children, to nine generations.

In the minds of his nomads, nothing was more desirable than to be one of the fellowship of *tar-khans*. They were fired by victory, by the rampaging of those three years through new lands, and for the nonce they were held in check by awe of the Mongol khan.

But around the person of the conqueror were gathered the wildest spirits of all Asia, the Turko-Mongol warriors from the sea to the T'ian shan where Gutchluk would soon rule Black Cathay (Kara K'itai). For the moment clan feuds were forgotten. Buddhist and *shaman*, devil-worshipper and Mohammedan and Nestorian Christian sat down as brothers, awaiting events.

Almost anything could have happened. What did happen was that the Mongol khan rose above the limitations of his ancestors. He called together the *kurultai*, the council of the khans, to select a single man to rule all the peoples of high Asia. An emperor.

He explained to them that they must choose one of their number to have authority over the others. Naturally enough, after the events of the last three years, the choice of the *kurultai* fell upon Temujin. More than that, the council decided that he was to have a fitting title. A soothsayer in the gathering now came forward and announced that his new name should be *Genghis Kha Khan*, the Greatest of Rulers, the Emperor of All Men.

The council was pleased, and at the unanimous insistence of the khans Temujin assumed his new title.

CHAPTER VII

THE YASSA

THE council had been held in 1206, and in the same year the official of Cathay, the Warden of the Western Marches, whose duty it was to watch over the barbarians beyond the great wall and collect tribute from them, reported that "absolute quiet prevails in the far kingdoms." Following the election of Genghis Khan as their master, the Turko-Mongol peoples were united for the first time in several centuries.

In the high tide of their enthusiasm they believed that Temujin, now Genghis Khan, was in reality a *bogdo*, a sending from the gods, endowed with the power of high Heaven. But no enthusiasm could have held these lawless hordes in restraint. They had lived too long governed by tribal custom. And customs vary as much as the natures of men.

To hold them in check, Genghis Khan had the military organization of his Mongols, most of whom were now veterans. But he announced that he had made the *Yassa*, to rule them. The *Yassa* was his code of laws, a combination of his own will and the most expedient of tribal customs.*

He made it clear that he disliked particularly theft and adultery, which were to be punished by death.

* See Note III, The Laws of Genghis Khan, page 214.

If a horse were stolen the punishment should be death. He said that it angered him to hear of a child disobedient to its parents, of the younger brother to the older ; a husband's want of confidence in his wife, a wife's lack of submission to her husband ; the failure of the rich to aid the poor and of inferiors to show respect for leaders.

Regarding strong drink, a Mongol failing, he said : " A man who is drunk is like one struck on the head ; his wisdom and skill avail him not at all. Get drunk only three times a month. It would be better not to get drunk at all. But who can abstain altogether ? "

Another weakness of the Mongols was fear of thunder. During the severe storms of the Gobi this fear had so overmastered them at times that they threw themselves into lakes and rivers to escape the wrath of the skies—at least, so the worthy voyager, Fra Rubruquis tells us. The *Yassa* forbade bathing or touching water at all during a thunderstorm.

Himself a man of violent rages, Genghis Khan denied his people their most cherished indulgence, violence. The *Yassa* interdicted quarrels among Mongols. On another point he was inexorable—there should be no other Genghis Kha Khan. His name and the names of his sons were written only in gilt, or were not written at all. Nor would the men of the new emperor willingly speak the name of the Khan.

A deist himself, raised among the ragged and rascally *shamans* of the Gobi, his code treated matters of religion indulgently. Leaders of other faiths, devotees, the criers of the mosques were to be freed from public charges. Indeed, a motley array of priest-

hood trailed after the Mongol camps—wandering
yellow and red lamas swinging their prayer wheels,
some of them wearing " stoles, painted with a likeness
of the true Christian devil "—thus Fra Rubruquis.
And Marco Polo relates that before a battle Genghis
Khan demanded that astrologers take the omens. The
" Saracen " soothsayers failed to prophesy effectively,
but the Nestorian Christians had better success with
two little canes marked with the names of the rival
leaders, which fell one on top of the other when lines
from the book of Psalms were read aloud. Though
Genghis Khan may have listened to the soothsayers
—and he listened attentively to the warnings of a
Cathayan astrologer in later life—he does not seem
to have turned back from any venture on account of
them.

The *Yassa* dealt in simple fashion with spies,
sodomites, false witnesses and black sorcerers. They
were put to death.

The first law of the *Yassa* is rather remarkable.
" It is ordered that all men should believe in one
God, creator of Heaven and earth, the sole giver of
goods and poverty, of life and death as pleases Him,
whose power over all things is absolute." An echo
here of the teachings of the early Nestorians. But this
law was never pronounced publicly. Genghis Khan
had no wish to make a dividing line among his subjects,
or to stir up the always latent embers of doctrinal
antagonism.

A psychologist might say that the *Yassa* aimed at
three things—obedience to Genghis Khan, a binding
together of the nomad clans, and the merciless punishment of wrong-doing. It concerned itself with men,

not property. And a man, by the way, was not to be adjudged guilty—unless caught in the act of crime—if he did not confess. It must be remembered that among the Mongols, an illiterate people, a man's spoken word was a solemn matter.

More often than not a nomad, faced with an accusation of wrong-doing, would admit it if he were guilty. There were instances of some who came in to the Khan and asked to be punished.

In the later years of his life, obedience to the Khan was absolute. The general of a division stationed a thousand miles from the court submitted to be relieved of his command and executed at the order of the Khan brought by a common courier.

" They are obedient to their lords beyond any other people," said the stout Fra Carpini, " giving them vast reverence and never deceiving them in word or action. They seldom quarrel, and brawls, wounds or slaying hardly ever happen. Thieves and robbers are nowhere found, so that their houses and carts in which all their goods and treasure rest are never locked or barred. If any animal of their herds go astray, the finder leaves it or drives it back to the officers who have charge of strays. Among themselves they are courteous and though victuals are scarce, they share them freely. They are very patient under privations, and though they may have fasted for a day or two, will sing and make merry. In journeying they bear cold or heat without complaining. They never fall out and though often drunk, never quarrel in their cups."

(This was a matter, apparently, of some surprise to the voyager out of Europe.)

"Drunkenness is honourable among them. When a

man has drunk to excess and vomits, he begins again to drink. Toward other people they are exceedingly proud and overbearing, looking upon all other men, however noble, with contempt. For we saw in the emperor's court the great duke of Russia, the son of the king of Georgia, and many sultans and other great men who had no honour or respect. Indeed, even the Tatars appointed to attend them, however low their condition, always went before these high-born captives and took the upper places.

" They are irritable and disdainful to other men, and beyond belief deceitful. Whatever mischief they intend they carefully conceal, that no one may provide against it. And the slaughter of other people they consider as nothing."

To aid one another—and destroy other people. An echo of the *Yassa*. These clansmen, war-hungry and smarting from ancient feuds, could be held together only in one way. Left to their own devices they would soon have been at their old work of mutual extermination, fighting for spoil and pasture land. The red-haired Kha Khan had sown the wind and stood to reap the whirlwind.

He realized this—he must have realized it, judging by his next actions. He had been weaned among the nomads and he knew that the one way to keep them from each other's throats was to lead them to war elsewhere. He meant to harness the whirlwind and direct it away from the Gobi.

The chronicle gives us a glimpse of him at this time, before the long feasting of the *kuriltai* came to an end. Standing at the foot of the mountain that shadowed his homeland, standing beneath the now familiar standard pole with its nine white yak-tails, he addressed the Bourchikoun and the chieftains who had pledged allegiance to him.

"These men who will share with me the good and bad of the future, whose loyalty will be like the clear rock crystal—I wish them to be called Mongols. Above everything that breathes on earth I wish them to be raised to power."

He had the imagination to see this assemblage of unbridled spirits united in one horde. The wise and mysterious Ugurs, the stalwart Karaïts, the hardy Yakka Mongols, the ferocious Tatars, the dour Merkits—the silent and long-enduring men from the snow tundras, the hunters of game—all the riders of high Asia, gathered into a single gigantic clan, himself the chieftain.

They had been united before, briefly, under the Hiung-nu monarchs who harried Cathay until the great wall was built to shut them out. Genghis Khan had the gift of eloquence to stir deep-seated emotions in them. And he never doubted his ability to lead them.

He held before their eyes the vision of conquest throughout unknown lands, but he exerted himself to the utmost to mobilize this new horde. He invoked the *Yassa*.

It was forbidden for any warrior of the horde to forsake his comrades—the men of his " ten." Or for the others of the " ten " to leave behind them a wounded man. Likewise was it forbidden any of the horde to flee before the standard withdrew from a battle, or to turn aside to pillage before permission was given by the officer commanding.

(The inevitable inclination of the man in the ranks to loot whenever possible was met by the rule that they were entitled to all they found—officers notwithstanding.)

And the observant Fra Carpini is authority that Genghis Khan enforced this portion of the *Yassa*, for he describes the Mongols as " never leaving the field while the standard was lifted, and never asking quarter if taken, or sparing a living foe."

The horde itself was no haphazard gathering of clans. Like the Roman legion it had its permanent organization, its units of ten to ten thousand—the *tuman* that formed a division, needless to say of cavalry. In command of the armies were the Orkhons, the marshals of the Khan, the infallible Subotai, the old and experienced Muhuli, and the fiery Chepé Noyon—eleven in all.

The weapons—at least the lances, heavy armour and shields—of the horde were kept in arsenal by certain officers, cared for and cleaned until the warriors were summoned for a campaign, when they were issued weapons, mustered and inspected by *gur-khans*. The sagacious Mongol did not intend to have several hundred thousand men loose and fully armed, scattered over a million square miles of plains and mountains.

To divert the energies of his horde, the *Yassa* ordered the winter—between the first heavy snow and the first grass—to be devoted to hunts on a grand scale, expeditions after antelope, deer and the fleet-footed wild ass.

In the spring he announced that councils would be

held, and all the higher officers were expected to attend. "Those who, instead of coming to me to hear my instructions, remain absent in their cantonments, will have the fate of a stone that is dropped into deep water, or an arrow among reeds—they will disappear."

No doubt Genghis Khan had learned from ancestral tradition, and had availed himself of existing customs ; but the creation of the horde as a permanent military organization was his work. The *Yassa* ruled it, the lash of inexorable authority held it together. Genghis Khan had under his hand a new force in warfare, a disciplined mass of heavy cavalry capable of swift movement in all kinds of country. Before his time the ancient Persians and the Parthians had perhaps as numerous bodies of cavalry, yet they lacked the Mongols' destructive skill with the bow and savage courage.

In the horde he had a weapon capable of vast destruction if rightly handled and held in restraint. And he had fully determined to wield it against Cathay, the ancient and unchanging empire behind the great wall.[*]

---

[*] See Note IV, The Numerical Strength of the Mongol Horde, page 218.

Part II

CHAPTER VIII

CATHAY

BEYOND the Great Wall things were vastly different from those in high Asia. Here existed a civilization of some five thousand years, with written records extending back thirty centuries. And here lived men who spent their lives in contemplation as well as in fighting.

Once the ancestors of these men had been nomads, a horse-riding people, adept in the use of the bow. But, for three thousand years, instead of migrating they had built cities, and much may be done in that time. They had multiplied enormously, and when men increase and crowd one another they build walls. And they divide themselves into different classes of human beings.

Unlike the Gobi, the men behind the great wall were slaves and peasants—scholars, soldiers, and beggars—mandarins, dukes and princes. Always they had had an emperor, the son of Heaven, *T'ien tsi,* and a court, the Clouds of Heaven.

In the year 1210, the Year of the Sheep in the Calendar of the Twelve Beasts, the throne was occupied by the Chin or Golden dynasty. The court was at Yen-king, near the site of modern Peking.

Cathay was like an aged woman, sunk in medita-
tion, clad perhaps in too elaborate garments, surrounded
by many children, little heeded.   The hours of its
rising and sleeping were all ordained ; it went forth in
chariots, attended by servants, and prayed to the
tablets of the dead.

Its garments were of floss silk, many-coloured—
though the slaves might run barefoot and cotton-clad.
Over the heads of its high officials umbrellas were
carried.   Inside the entrances of its dwellings, screens
served to keep out wandering devils.   It bowed the
head to ritual, and studied how to make its conduct
perfect.

Barbarians had come down from the north—the
Cathayans themselves, and the Chins, a century ago.
They had been absorbed into the great mass of human
beings behind the wall.   In time they had fallen into
the manners of Cathay, clad themselves in its garments and followed its ritual.

Within the cities of Cathay were pleasure lakes,
and barges where men could sit with rice wine,
listening to the melody of silver bells in a woman's
hand. They might, perhaps, drift under a tiled pagoda
roof, or hear the summons of a temple gong.

They studied the Bamboo Books written in forgotten ages and discussed together at long-drawn
feasts the golden days of T'ang. They were the men
of Chin, followers of a dynasty, servants of the sitter
on the throne. Tradition ruled them, as it taught
them the highest duty was to the dynasty.   Even
though they might, as in the days of Master K'ung,*
cry out at the imperial cortège wherein the emperor

* Confucius.

rode with a courtesan in a carriage before the savant, " Lo, here is lust in front and virtue behind."

Or even a vagabond poet, wrapped in drunken contemplation of the beauty of moonlight upon a river, might fall in the water and be drowned and be no less a poet for all that. The pursuit of perfection is a laborious business, but time did not matter much in Cathay.

A painter contented himself with touching silk with a bit of colour—a bird on a branch, or a snow-capped mountain. A detail, but a perfect detail. The astrologer in his roof among the brass globes and quadrants, noted down each movement of a star ; the minstrel of war was contemplative.

" *No sound of a bird now breaks from the hushed walls. Only the wind whistles through the long night, where ghosts of the dead wander in the gloom. The fading moon twinkles on the falling snow. The fosses of the walls are frozen with blood and bodies with beards stiff with ice. Each arrow is spent ; every bow-string broken. The strength of the war horse is lost. Thus is the city of Han-li under the hand of the enemy.*"

So the minstrel, seeing a picture in death itself, voiced the resignation that is the heritage of Cathay.

War engines they had—twenty horse chariots, ancient and useless, but also stone casters, cross-bows that the strength of ten men did not serve to wind— catapults of which it took two hundred artillerists to draw taut the massive ropes ; they had the " Fire that Flies " and the fire that could be exploded in bamboo tubes.

The waging of war had been an art in Cathay, since the days when the armoured regiments and chariots manœuvred over the wastes of Asia, and a temple was erected in the camp for the general commanding to meditate upon his plans undisturbed. Kwan-ti, the war god, never lacked devotees. The strength of Cathay was in the discipline of its trained masses, and its enormous reservoirs of human life. As to its weakness, a Cathayan general seventeen centuries ago had written ominously :

"A ruler can bring misfortune upon his army by attempting to govern it like a kingdom, when he is ignorant of the conditions faced by the army and within it. This is called hobbling an army. This causes restlessness among the soldiers.

"And when an army is restless and distrustful, anarchy results and victory is thrown away."

The weakness of Cathay was in its emperor, who must remain in Yen-king and leave matters of leadership to his generals ; and the strength of the nomads beyond the wall was in the military genius of their khan, who led the army in person.

The case of Genghis Khan was very like that of Hannibal in Italy. He had a limited number of warriors. A single decisive defeat would send the nomads back into their deserts. A doubtful victory would be no gain. His success must be decisive without too great a loss in man-power. And he would be called upon to manœuvre his divisions against armies led by masters of tactics.

Meanwhile, out in Karakorum, he was still the "Commander Against Rebels," still the subject of the Golden Emperor.

In the past when the fortunes of Cathay had been ascendant, the emperors had demanded tribute of the nomads beyond the great wall. In moments of weakness the dynasties of Cathay had bought off the nomads, sending them such things as silver, floss silk, worked leather, carved jade and caravan loads of grain and wine, to keep them from raiding. To manifest its honour, or, in other words, to save its face, the dynasty of Cathay would call these payments gifts. But in the years of power the payments demanded from the nomad khans were called tribute.

The predatory tribes had not forgotten these magnificent gifts, nor the annoying exactions of Cathayan officials and the rare expeditions of the " hat and girdle " people from the barrier of the great wall. Thus the peoples of the eastern Gobi were at the present moment nominally subjects of the Golden Emperor, administered—in theory—by the absentee Warden of the Western Marches. Genghis Khan was entered in the roll of officials as " Commander Against Rebels." In due course the scribes of Yen-king, combing over the records, sent emissaries to him to collect tribute of horses and cattle. This tribute he did not pay.

The situation, you will perceive, was typically Chinese. The attitude of Genghis Khan may be described in two words—watchful waiting.

In the course of his campaigns within the Gobi, he had encountered the great wall and considered attentively this rampart of brick and stone with its towers over the gates and its impressive summit upon which six horsemen could gallop abreast.

More recently, he had caused his standard to be displayed from gate to gate along its nearest circuit— a circumstance to which the Warden of the Western Marches and the Golden Emperor paid not the slightest attention. But the frontier tribes, the buffer peoples, living within the shadow of the wall and serving the monarch of Cathay upon his hunting excursions, took full notice of this bold act and decided among themselves that the Golden Emperor was afraid of the nomad chieftain.

This was hardly the case. Secure within their walled cities, the millions of Cathay thought not at all of the horde of a quarter million warriors. Except that the Golden Emperor, in the course of his continual warfare with the ancient house of Sung in the south beyond the Son of the Ocean, the Yang-tze, sent other emissaries to the Mongols to request the assistance of the nomad horsemen.

Several *tumans* were lent by Genghis Khan, quite readily. Chepé Noyon and others of the Orkhons commanded these cavalry divisions. What they effected on behalf of the Golden Emperor is unknown. But they used their eyes and asked questions.

They had all the nomad's ability to remember landmarks. And when they rode back to the horde in the Gobi they had a pretty good idea of the topography of Cathay.

They brought with them, also, tales of wonders. In Cathay, they said, the roads ran clear across the rivers, on stone platforms ; wooden *kibitkas* floated on the rivers ; all the largest cities had walls too high for a horse to leap.

Men in Cathay wore vests of nankeen and silks of all colours, and even some of the slaves had as many as seven vests. Instead of old minstrels, young poets entertained the court—not by droning hero legends but by writing words on a silk screen. And these words described the beauty of women. It was all very wonderful.

His officers were eager to launch themselves at the great wall. To have gratified them, to have led his wild clans at that time against Cathay would have meant disaster for the Khan, and calamity at home as well. If he left his new empire and suffered defeat in the east, in Cathay, other enemies would not hesitate at all to invade the Mongol dominion.

The Gobi desert was his, but he could look south, south-west and west and see there formidable foes. Along the *Nan-lu*, the southern caravan track, existed the curious kingdom of Hia—the so-called robber kingdom. Here were lean and predatory Tibetans, come down from the hills to plunder, and outlawed Cathayans. Beyond them extended the power of Black Cathay, a kind of mountain empire, and to the west, the roving hordes of Kirghiz who had kept out of the way of the Mongols.

Against all these troublesome neighbours, Genghis Khan sent portions of his horde, mounted divisions commanded by the Orkhons. He himself rode several seasons to war in the Hia country—a war of raids in open country that convinced the Hia chieftains it would be well to make peace with him. The peace was strengthened by a blood tie—one of the women of the royal family being sent to Genghis Khan for a wife. Other ties were made in the west. All this was caution—in military parlance, clearing his flanks. But it won him allies among the chieftains and recruits for the horde. And it gave the horde itself some very desirable experience in campaigning.

Meanwhile the monarch of Cathay died ; his son was seated on the dragon throne, a son tall and superbly bearded, interested chiefly in painting and hunting. He called himself Wai Wang, an imposing title for a commonplace man.

In due course the mandarins of Cathay got out the tribute rolls for the new monarch, and an officer was sent into the plateaus of the Gobi to collect tribute from Genghis Khan. He took with him also the proclamation of the new sovereign, Wai Wang. This, an imperial edict, should have been received on bended knees, but the Mongol stretched out his hand for it and remained standing, nor did he give it to an interpreter to read.

"Who is the new emperor?" he asked.

"Wai Wang."

Instead of inclining his head toward the south, the Khan spat. "I thought the son of Heaven should be an extraordinary man; but an imbecile like Wai Wang is unworthy a throne. Why should I humiliate myself before him?"

With that he mounted his horse and rode away. That night the Orkhons were summoned to his pavilion, with his new allies, the Idikut of the Swooping Hawks, and the Lion Lord of the western Turks. The next day the envoy was called before the Khan and given a message to take back to the Golden Emperor.

"Our dominion," said the Mongol, "is now so well ordered that we can visit Cathay. Is the dominion of the Golden Khan so well ordered that he can receive us? We will go with an army that is like a roaring ocean. It matters not whether we are met with friendship or war. If the Golden Khan chooses to be our friend, we will allow him the government under us of his dominion; if he chooses war, it will last until one of us is victor, one defeated."

No more insulting message could have been sent. Genghis Khan must have decided that the moment for invasion was at hand. While the old emperor lived he had felt bound, perhaps, by feudal allegiance to Cathay. With Wai Wang he had no concern.

The envoy returned to Yen-king where the court of Wai Wang resided. Wai Wang was angered by the response he brought with him.* The Warden of the Western Marches was asked what the Mongols were about. He replied that they were making many arrows and gathering horses. Thereupon, the Warden of the Western Marches was clapped into prison.

The winter was passing and the Mongols went on making many arrows and gathering horses. Unfortunately for the Golden Emperor, they did much more than that. Genghis Khan sent envoys and presents to the men of Liao-tung in the northern part of Cathay. He knew that these were warlike spirits who had not forgotten their conquest by a previous Golden Emperor.

This envoy met the prince of the Liao dynasty and a compact was sworn between them, and blood drawn and arrows broken to bind it. The men of Liao— literally the men of Iron—would invade the north of Cathay, and the Mongol Khan would restore to them all their old possessions; a compact, by the way, that Genghis Khan kept to the letter. Eventually he made the princes of Liao the rulers of Cathay, under himself.

---

* Some accounts have it that a Chin army was sent against the nearest of the Gobi clans, and this is very probably so, because we find the Mongols fighting outside the wall before their advance into the Chin empire.

CHAPTER IX

THE GOLDEN EMPEROR

FOR the first time the nomad horde was moving to the invasion of a civilized power of much greater military strength. We are able to see Genghis Khan at work in the field of war.*

The first of the horde had been sent out of the Gobi long since—spies and warriors who were to capture and bring back informers. These were already behind the great wall.

Next went the advance points, some two hundred riders scattered over the countryside in pairs. Far behind these scouts came the advance, some thirty thousand picked warriors on good horses—at least two horses to a man—three *tumans*, commanded by the veteran Muhuli, the fiery Chepé Noyon and that surprising youngster Subotai, the Masséna of the Khan's marshals.

In close touch by courier with this advance, the main body of the horde came over the barren plateaus, rolling up the dust clouds. A hundred thousand, mostly Yakka Mongols of long 'service, formed the centre, and the right and left wings numbered as many. Genghis Khan always commanded the centre, keeping his youngest son at his side for instruction.

Like Napoleon, he had his imperial guard, a

* See Note V, The Mongol Plan of Invasion, page 221.

thousand strong, mounted on black horses with leather armour. Probably in this first campaign of 1211 against Cathay, the horde was not in such strength.

It neared the great wall and passed through this barrier without delay or the loss of a man. Genghis Khan had been tampering for some time with the frontier clans, and one of the gates was opened to him by sympathizers.

Once within the wall the Mongol divisions separated, going into different parts of Shan-si and Chih-li. They had definite orders. They needed no transport and did not know the meaning of a base of supplies.

The first line of the Cathayan armies, mustered to guard the frontier roads, fared badly. The Mongol cavalry divisions nosed out the scattered forces of the Emperor, composed mainly of foot soldiers, and rode them down, making havoc with arrows shot from the back of a hard-running horse into the close packed ranks of infantry.

One of the main armies of the Emperor, feeling its way toward the invaders, wavered among a labyrinth of gorges and small hills. The general in command, newly appointed, did not know the country and had to ask his way of peasants. Chepé Noyon, moving toward him, remembered very well the roads and valleys of this district, and actually made a night march around the Chin forces, taking them in the rear the following day. This army was terribly cut up by the Mongols, and the remnants of it, fleeing east, brought fear to the largest of the Chin armies.

This wavered in turn, and its general fled toward the capital. Genghis Khan reached Taitong-fu, the first of the large walled cities and invested it, then hurried on his divisions toward the reigning city, Yen-king.

The devastation wrought by the horde and its nearness filled Wai Wang with alarm, and this sitter on the dragon throne would have fled from Yen-king if his ministers had not restrained him. The greatest defence of the empire was now rallying to Wai Wang as it always has in China when the nation was menaced —the innumerable multitudes of the middle-class, the stolid and devoted throngs, scions of warlike ancestors, who knew no higher duty than to uphold the throne.

Genghis Khan had broken down the first armed resistance of Cathay with amazing rapidity. His divisions had captured a number of cities, though Taitong-fu, the Western Court, still held out.

But he was faced, as Hannibal before Rome, with the real vitality of a stout-hearted domain. New armies appeared up the great rivers ; the garrisons of beleaguered cities seemed to multiply. He passed through the outer gardens of Yen-king itself and beheld for the first time the stupendous extent of lofty walls, the hills and bridges and mounting roofs of a whole series of citadels.

He must have seen the uselessness of laying siege to such a place, with his small numbers, because he drew back at once, and when autumn came he ordered his standards back to the Gobi.

In the following spring when his horses were restored to strength he appeared again within the wall. He found the towns that had surrendered to him in the first campaign were now garrisoned and defiant, and he set to work anew. The Western Court was invested again and here he now kept the horde entire.

Apparently he used the siege as a kind of bait, waiting for the armies that were sent to relieve it and cutting them up as they came. The war made manifest two things: the Mongol cavalry could out-manœuvre and destroy Cathayan armies in the field, but could not as yet take strong cities.

Chepé Noyon, however, managed to do this very thing. Their allies, the Liao princes, were hard beset by sixty thousand Cathayans up in the north, and appealed to the Khan for aid. He sent Chepé Noyon with a *tuman*, and the energetic Mongol general laid siege to Liao-yang itself in the rear of the Cathayan forces.

The first efforts of the Mongols failed to gain them anything and Chepé Noyon, who was as impatient as Marshal Ney, essayed a ruse that Genghis Khan had used in the field, though not in siege work. He abandoned his baggage, carts and supplies in full sight of the Cathayans, and drew off with his horse herds as if giving up the struggle or fearing the approach of a relieving army.

For two days the Mongols rode away slowly, then shifted to their best horses and galloped back swiftly in a single night, "the sword in the rein hand." They arrived before Liao-yang at daybreak. The Cathayans, convinced that the Mongols had retired, were occupied in plundering the baggage and carrying it within the walls—all gates open and the townspeople mingled with the warriors. The unexpected onset of the nomads took them completely by surprise, and the result was a terrible massacre followed by the storming of Liao-yang.

Chepé Noyon recovered all his own baggage and a good deal more.

But in pressing the siege of the Western Court, Genghis Khan was wounded. His horde withdrew from Cathay, as the tide ebbs from the shore, bearing him with it.

Every autumn it was necessary for them to go back. Fresh horses must be gathered together. During the summer they had foraged—men and beasts—on the country, but a winter in north China would not yield enough sustenance to the horde. Besides, there were warlike neighbours to be kept at a distance.

The next season Genghis Khan did no more than launch a few raids—enough to keep the Cathayans from resting too much.

The war, his first on a grand scale, had fallen into stalemate. Unlike Hannibal, he could not leave garrisons in the captured cities of the empire. His Mongols, unaccustomed to fighting at that time from behind walls, would have been annihilated by the Cathayans during the winter.

A series of victories in the field, gained by screening the movements of his squadrons and uniting them by swift marches against the Cathayan armies, had resulted only in driving the enemy forces within walls. He had come within sight of Yen-king itself, in his effort to get at the Emperor ; but the master of the Chin could not be driven from the nearly impregnable citadel. Meanwhile the Chin armies were prevailing against the men of Liao-tung, and the riders of Hia who were supporting the flanks of the Khan.

Under the circumstances, a nomad chieftain would have been expected to let well enough alone, and to

remain outside the great wall with his booty of the
past seasons and the prestige of victories gained over
the great Chin power. But Genghis Khan, wounded
and still inexorable, was gaining experience and
profiting by it, while foreboding began to prey upon
the Golden Emperor.

Foreboding grew to fear when the first grass came
in the spring of 1214. Three Mongol armies invaded
Cathay from different points. On the south the three
sons of the Khan cut a wide swathe across Shan-si ;
on the north Juchi crossed the Khingan range and
joined forces with the men of Liao-tung ; meanwhile
Genghis Khan with the centre of the horde reached
the shore of the great ocean behind Yen-king.

These three armies operated in a new fashion. They
remained separated ; they settled down to the siege
of the strongest cities, gathering the folk from the
countryside and driving the captives before them in
the first storm. More often than not the Cathayans
within the walls opened their gates. At such times,
they were spared their lives, even while everything in
the open country was annihilated or driven off—crops
trampled and burned, herds taken up, and men,
women and children cut down.

Confronted by this war à outrance, several Cathayan generals went over to the Mongols with their
commands, and were installed with other officers of
Liao-tung in the captured cities.

Famine and disease, two of the four horsemen of
the Apocalypse, followed upon the heels of the Mongol
riders. Across the sky-line passed the train-bands of
the horde, the endless carts, the bullock herds, the
horned standards.

As the season drew to its close, disease took its toll of the horde. The horses were weak, ill-conditioned. Genghis Khan with the centre of the horde camped near the battlements of Yen-king and his officers begged him to assault the city.

Again he refused, but he sent a message to the Golden Emperor.

"What do you think now of the war between us? All the provinces north of the Yellow River are in my power. I am going to my homeland. But could you permit my officers to go away without sending gifts to appease them?"

A request extraordinary on the face of it, but a simple stroke of policy on the part of the matter-of-fact Mongol. If the Golden Emperor granted his demand, he would have the gifts to reward his officers and satisfy their restlessness, and the prestige of the dragon throne would suffer greatly.

Some of the Cathayan councillors who knew the enfeebled condition of the horde besought the Emperor to lead out the forces in Yen-king against the Mongols. What result this would have had, there is no telling. But the Chin monarch had suffered too much to act boldly. He sent out to Genghis Khan five hundred youths and as many girl slaves, with a herd of fine horses and loads of silk and gold. A truce was agreed on, and the Chins pledged themselves to allow the allies of the Khan, the Liao princes, to remain unmolested in Liao-tung.

More than that, the Khan demanded—if there was to be a truce between them—that he be given a wife of the imperial blood. And this lady of the reigning family was sent to him.

Genghis Khan did turn back to the Gobi that autumn, but on the edge of the desert he slew the multitude of captives that had been carried along by the horde—an act of unprovoked cruelty.

(It appears to have been a custom of the Mongols to put to death all captives, except artisans and savants, when they turned their faces homeward after a campaign. Few, if any, slaves appear in the native lands of the Mongols at this time. A throng of ill-nourished captives on foot could not have crossed the lengths of the barrens that surrounded the home of the nomads. Instead of turning them loose, the Mongols made an end of them—as we might cast off old garments. Human life had no value in the eyes of the Mongols, who desired only to depopulate fertile lands to provide grazing for their herds. It was their boast at the end of the war against Cathay that a horse could be ridden without stumbling across the sites of many cities of Cathay.)

Whether Genghis Khan would have left Cathay in peace is uncertain. But the Golden Emperor acted on his own account. Leaving his eldest son in Yen-king, he fled south.

" *We* announce to our subjects that we shall change our residence to the capital of the south."

Thus the imperial decree—a weak gesture to preserve his honour. His councillors, the governors of Yen-king, the elder Chin nobles, all besought him not to abandon his people. But go he did, and rebellion followed upon his flight.

CHAPTER X

THE RETURN OF THE MONGOLS

WHEN he fled with his *entourage* from the imperial city, the Chin Emperor left in the palace his son, the heir apparent. He did not wish to abandon the heart of his country without keeping in Yen-king some semblance of rule, some individual of the dynasty for the people to see. Yen-king was strongly garrisoned.

But the chaos foreseen by the elder nobles now began to break up the armed forces of the Chins. Some of the troops escorting the Emperor mutinied and went off to join the Mongols.

In the imperial city itself a curious revolt took place. The hereditary princes, the officials and mandarins assembled and vowed fresh allegiance to the dynasty. Deserted by their monarch, they resolved to carry on the war themselves. Thronging into the streets, bareheaded in the rain, the stalwart soldiery of Cathay pledged itself to follow the fortunes of the Chin heir apparent and the nobles. The old and deep spirit of loyalty manifested itself again in this moment, brought to the surface, as it were, by the flight of a weak ruler.

The Emperor sent couriers to Yen-king to recall his son to the south.

" Do not do that ! " the elder Chins protested.

But the Emperor was obstinate, and his wish was

Chepé Noyon was sent at a gallop back to the Gobi, to quiet the chieftains at home.

Genghis Khan detached Subotai to go and look at the situation. This Orkhon disappeared from view for some months, sending back only routine reports as to the condition of his horses. He found, apparently, nothing worth while in northern Cathay, because he returned to the horde bearing with him the submission of Korea. Left to his own devices he had kept quiet and had circled the gulf of Liao-tung to explore a new country. This disposition to wander, when he was given an independent command, brought calamity to Europe in a later day.

The Khan himself remained with the nucleus of the horde near the great wall. He was fifty-five years of age ; his grandson Kubilai had been born, back in the pavilions—no longer the felt *yurts*—of the Gobi. His sons were grown men ; but in this crisis he gave the command of his divisions to the Orkhons, the proved leaders of the horde, the men who could do no wrong and whose descendants, by virtue of their ability, were never to suffer want or punishment. He had taught Chepé Noyon and Subotai how to handle mounted divisions, and he had tested the veteran Muhuli.

So Genghis Khan remained a spectator of the downfall of Cathay sitting in his tent, listening to the reports of the gallopers who rode to him without dismounting to cook food or to sleep.

It was Muhuli aided by Mingan, a prince of Liao-tung, who directed the thrust at Yen-king. With no more than five thousand Mongols at his heels, he retraced his steps eastward, gathering as he went a multitude of Cathayan deserters and wandering bands of warriors. Subotai hovering on his flank, he pitched his tents before the outer walls of Yen-king.

With men enough in Yen-king to have endured a siege successfully, and with ample stock of weapons and all the paraphernalia of war, the Cathayans were too disorganized to hold out. When fighting began in the suburbs one of the Chin generals deserted. The women of the imperial household who begged to go with him, he left behind in the darkness. Looting began in the merchants' streets, and the unfortunate women wandered hopelessly among bands of shouting and frightened soldiery.

Fire followed, springing up in various parts of the city. In the palace, eunuchs and slaves were to be seen flitting through the corridors, their arms filled with gold and silver ornaments. The hall of audience was deserted, and the sentries left their posts to join the pillagers.

Wang-Yen, the other general commanding, a prince of the blood, had received not so long ago a decree from the departed Emperor, pardoning all criminals and prisoners in Cathay and increasing the gifts to the soldiers. A futile last measure, it availed the solitary Wang-Yen not at all.

Matters being hopeless, the general commanding prepared to die as custom required. He retired to his chambers and wrote a petition to his Emperor, acknowledging himself guilty and worthy of death in that he had not been able to defend Yen-king.

This valediction, as it might be called, he wrote on the lapel of his robe. Then he called in his servants and divided all his garments and wealth among them. Ordering the mandarin who attended him to prepare a cup of poison, he continued writing.

Then Wang-Yen asked his friend to leave the chamber, and drank the poison. Yen-king was in flames, and the Mongols rode in upon a scene of defenceless terror.

The methodical Muhuli, indifferent to the passing of a dynasty, occupied himself with collecting and sending to the Khan the treasure and the munitions of the city.

Among the captive officers sent to the Khan was a prince of Liao-tung who had been serving the Cathayans. He was tall and bearded to the waist, and the Khan's attention was caught by his deep, clear voice. He asked the captive's name and learned that it was Ye Liu Chutsai.

" Why didst thou abide with the dynasty that was the old enemy of thy family ? " Genghis Khan asked.

" My father was a servant to the Chin, and others of my family also," the young prince replied. " It was not fitting that I should do otherwise."

This pleased the Mongol.

" Well hast thou served thy former master, and so thou canst serve me with trust. Be one among mine."

Some others who had deserted the dynasty he caused to be put to death, believing that they were not to be relied upon. It was Ye Liu Chutsai who said to him afterward ; " Thou hast conquered a great empire in the saddle. Thou canst not govern it so."

Whether the victorious Mongol saw the truth of this, or realized that in the learned Cathayans he had instruments as important as their war engines capable of casting stones and fire, he permitted himself to be advised. He appointed governors for the conquered districts of Cathay from among the Liao-tung men.

CHAPTER XI

UNLIKE other conquerors, Genghis Khan did not settle down in the most luxurious part of his new dominion, Cathay. When he rode through the great wall after the fall of the Chins, he did not return. He left Muhuli there as a war lord, and hastened back to the barren plateaus that were his birthright.

Here he had headquarters. Of the desert cities, he selected Karakorum, the Black Sands, as his *ordu*.

And here he assembled everything that a nomad could desire. A strange city, Karakorum, a metropolis of the barrens, wind-swept and sand-whipped. The dwellings, dried mud and thatch, arranged without any thought of streets. Around it, the domes of black felt *yurts*.

The years of privation and of wandering were past. Vast stables housed in winter picked herds of horses bearing the Khan's brand. Granaries guarded against famine—millet and rice for men, hay for the horses. Caravanserais sheltered travellers and visiting ambassadors who were flocking out of all northern Asia.

From the south came Arab and Turkish merchants. With them Genghis Khan established his own method of dealing. He did not like to haggle. If the merchants tried to bargain with him their goods were taken without payment ; if, on the other hand, they gave everything to the Khan, they received in return gifts that more than paid them.

Beside the district of the ambassadors was the quarter of the priests. Old Buddhist temples elbowed stone mosques and the small wooden churches of Nestorian Christians. Everyone was free to worship as he pleased as long as he obeyed the laws of the *Yassa*, and the rules of the Mongol camp.

Visitors were met by Mongol officers at the frontiers and forwarded to Karakorum with guides—word of their coming sent ahead by the busy couriers of the caravan routes. Once within sight of the grazing herds, the black domes of the *yurts*, and the rows of the *kibitkas* on the treeless and hill-less plain that surrounded the city of the Khan, they were taken in charge by the Master of Law and Punishment.

In obedience to an old custom of the nomads, they were made to pass between two large fires. No harm came to them as a rule, but the Mongols believed that if any deviltry were concealed in them the fires would scorch them. Then they were given quarters and food and—if the Khan signified his assent—were led into the presence of the Mongol conqueror.

He held his court within a high pavilion of white felt lined with silk. By the entrance stood a silver table set with mare's milk, fruit and meat, so that all who came to him could eat as much as they wished. On a dais at the far end of the pavilion sat the Khan on a low bench with Bourtai or another wife below him on the left side.

Few ministers attended him—Ye Liu Chutsai, per- haps, in his embroidered robes, majestic enough with his long beard and deep voice—a Ugur scribe with his roll of paper and brush—a Mongol *noyon*,*honorary cup-bearer. On benches around the walls of the pavilion other nobles sat in decorous silence, wearing the long wadded coats with hanging girdles, the uptilted white felt hats, the undress uniform of the horde. In the centre of the pavilion glowed a fire of thorns and dung.

Tar-khans, honoured above all others, might swagger in at will, and take their seat on the benches, their feet crossed under them, scarred hands resting on the stalwart thighs of horsemen. *Orkhons**†and divisional commanders might join them, carrying their maces. Conversation would be in low, drawling voices, and utter silence would prevail when the Khan spoke.

When he had said anything, that subject was closed. No man might add a word to his. Argument was a breach of manners—exaggeration a moral lapse, and lying a matter for the Master of Punishment. Words were few and painstakingly exact.

Strangers were expected to bring gifts with them. The gifts were taken in to the Khan before the visitors were passed in by the captain of that day's guard. Then the newcomers were searched for weapons and cautioned against touching the threshold of the pavilion, or any of the ropes—if it were a tent. To speak to the Khan they must first kneel. After they had presented themselves at this *ordu* they must not depart until told to do so by the Khan.

Karakorum—now vanished under the encroaching sands of the Gobi—was ruled by an iron will. Men

---

* *Noyon* or *notan*, commander of a *tuman* or division of ten thousand ; sometimes merely a noble.
*† *Orkhon*, or *Ur-khan*, commander of an army.

A Formal Audience at Karakorum, Illustrating a Seventeenth Century Artist's Conception of the Mongol Tent Wagons or Yurts

entering the *ordu* became servants of the Master of Thrones and Crowns. Other laws did not exist.

"On joining the Tatars," said the stout-hearted monk, Fra Rubruquis, "I thought myself entered into another world."

It was a world that moved by the laws of the *Yassa*, and awaited in silence the will of the Khan. The routine was all military—and the utmost of order prevailed. The pavilion of the Khan always faced south, and a space was left clear on this side. To right and left, as the children of Israel had their appointed places about the Tabernacle, the people of the horde had their fixed stations.

The household of the Khan had grown. In their tents, scattered through the *ordu*, waited upon by their own people, he had other women than Bourtai of the grey eyes. He had taken to wife princesses of Cathay and Liao, daughters of royal Turkish families and the most beautiful women of the desert clans.

He could appreciate beauty in women, not less than sagacity and hardihood in men, and swiftness and endurance in fine horses. Once the attractive face and bearing of a girl in a captured province were described to him by a Mongol who did not know just where she might be found. "If she is really beautiful," the Khan answered impatiently, "I will find her."

An amusing story is told of a dream that disturbed him—a dream that pictured one of his women plotting to harm him. At the time he was in the field, as usual, and when he waked he called out immediately: "Who is leader of the guard at the tent entrance?"

When the officer in question had spoken his name,

the Khan gave an order. " Such-and-such a woman is thine, as a gift. Take her to thy tent."

The matter of ethics he solved in a fashion all his own. Another concubine had yielded to the advances of a Mongol of his household. When he had pondered this, the Khan did not put either of the two to death, but sent them from his presence, saying, " I acted wrongly in taking to myself a girl of ignoble instincts."

Of all his sons he recognized as his heirs only the four born of Bourtai. They had been his chosen companions, and he had watched them, giving each a veteran officer as tutor. When he had satisfied himself as to their different nature and abilities he made them *Orluks*—Eagles—princes of the imperial blood. And they had their part to play in the orderly scheme of things.

Juchi the first-born was made Master of Hunting —from which the Mongols still gleaned a great part of their sustenance. Chatagai became Master of Law and Punishment ; Ogotai was Master of Counsel ; the youngest, Tuli, nominally chief of the army, the Khan kept at his side. Juchi, whose son Batu founded the Golden Horde that crushed Russia—Chatagai, who inherited Central Asia and whose descendant Babar was the first of the great Moghuls of India— Tuli, whose son Kubilai reigned from the China sea to mid-Europe.

The youthful Kubilai was a favourite of the Khan, who evinced toward him all the pride of a grand-father. " Mark well the words of the boy Kubilai ; they are full of wisdom."

Upon his return from Cathay, Genghis Khan

found the westerly half of his young empire highly demoralized. The powerful Turkish peoples of Central Asia, feudatories of the empire of Kara K'itai, had come under the hand of a gifted usurper, a certain Gutchluk, who was prince of the Naimans and had been defeated some time before by the Mongols after the battle with the Karaïts.

Gutchluk seems to have raised himself to fame by most profitable treachery. He allied himself with the still greater powers of the far west, and put to death his host, the Khan of Black Cathay. While Genghis Khan had been occupied beyond the great wall, he had disorganized the valuable Ugurs, and had slain the Christian khan of Almalyk, a subject of the Mongol. The always restless Merkits had left the horde and joined him.

With Gutchluk and his brief empire* in the wide ranges that extend from Tibet to Samarkand, Genghis Khan dealt decisively upon his return to Karakorum. The horde was remounted on fresh horses and led against the Naimans. The lord of Black Cathay was tricked out of position and soundly whipped by the veteran Mongols ; Subotai was detached with a division to bring the Merkits to their proper sense of duty, and Chepé Noyon was gratified with the command of two *yumans* and orders to hunt down Gutchluk and bring him back dead.

---

* Gutchluk's empire included what was later the heart of Tamerlane's dominion. The military operations that brought about the defeat of the Naimans and Kara K'itains were on a large scale They were brilliantly conceived and swiftly carried out As in the last campaign in China, the Khan entrusted the leadership of his divisions to his Orkhons and sons. It would be impossible without going into the complex political history of this region, with its changes from Ugur overlordship to Kirghiz and Cathayan rule, to emphasize fully the importance of its conquest by the Mongols.

With Chepé Noyon's adroit manœuvring among the ranges we need not concern ourselves. He met the zeal of the Mohammedans by offering amnesty to all foes except Gutchluk, and opened the gates of the Buddhist temples that had been closed by the war; then he chased the emperor of a year over the Roof of the World until Gutchluk was slain and his head sent back to Karakorum—with the herd of a thousand white-nosed horses that the energetic Mongol had been collecting on the side, as it were.

The affair—and it might have been disastrous to the Khan if he had lost that first battle—had two results. The nearest of the wild Turkish tribes, that stretched from Tibet across the heights to the steppes of Russia, became part of the horde. After the downfall of northern Cathay, these same nomads held what might be called the balance of power in Asia. The victorious Mongols were still a minority.

And the opening of the temples gave Genghis Khan new prestige. It was told from mountain city to valley camp that he had conquered Cathay, and the vast and shadowy influence of Buddhist Cathay was enveloped around his person. On the other hand, the discomfited mullahs were gratified that they were not molested and were freed of tithes and taxation. Under the snow summits of Tibet, within the fiercest amphitheatre of religious hatred in the world, bonze and mullah and lama were placed on an equal footing, and warned. The shadow of the *Yassa*. Envoys of the Khan—bearded Cathayans, intoning the new law of the conqueror, appeared to bring order out of chaos, even as they were struggling to bring relief to Cathay behind the iron willed Muhuli.

A courier galloped down the caravan tracks to the exultant Chepé Noyon, bringing word that the thousand horses had reached the Khan. " Do not become proud, through success ! "

Whether chastened or not, Chepé Noyon went on gathering warriors under the ranges of Tibet. Nor did he return to Karakorum. There was work ahead for him in another quarter of the world.

Meanwhile, with the overthrow of Gutchluk, an armistice as sudden and decisive as the fall of a curtain settled down on north Asia. From the China to the Aral sea one master reigned. Rebellion had ceased. The couriers of the Khan galloped over fifty degrees of longitude, and it was said that a virgin carrying a sack of gold could ride unharmed from one border of the nomad empire to the other.

But this administrative activity did not altogether satisfy the ageing conqueror. He no longer relished the winter hunts over the prairies. One day in the pavilion at Karakorum he asked an officer of the Mongol guard what, in all the world, could bring the greatest happiness.

" The open steppe, a clear day, and a swift horse under you," responded the officer after a little thought, " and a falcon on your wrist to start up hares."

" Nay," responded the Khan, " to crush your enemies, to see them fall at your feet—to take their horses and goods and hear the lamentation of their women. That is best."

The Master of Thrones and Crowns was also the Scourge. His next move was one of conquest, terrible in its effect, and it was toward the west. And it came about in a most curious way.

Part III

CHAPTER XII

THE SWORD-ARM OF ISLAM

UNTIL now the dominion of Genghis Khan had been confined to far Asia. He had grown up in his deserts and his first contact with civilization had been in Cathay.

And from the cities of Cathay he had gone back to the grazing lands of his native plains. More recently, the affair with Gutchluk, and the arrival of Mohammedan merchants had taught him something about the other half of Asia.

He knew now that beyond the ranges of his westerly border existed fertile valleys where snow never fell. Here, also, were rivers that never froze. Here multitudinous peoples lived in cities more ancient than Karakorum or Yen-king. And from these peoples of the west came the caravans that brought finely tempered steel blades and the best chain mail—white cloth and red leather, ambergris and ivory, turquoise and rubies.

To reach him, these caravans had to cross the barrier of mid-Asia, the network of mountain ranges that extended roughly north-east and south-west of the *Taghdumbash*, the Roof of the World. From time immemorable this mountain barrier had existed. It was the mountain Kâf of the early Arabs. It stood, vast and partially desolate, between the nomads of the Gobi and the rest of the world.

From time to time some of the nomad peoples had broken through the barrier, driven out by stronger nations still father east. The Huns and Avars had disappeared into the ranges, and had not come back.

And at intervals the conquerors of the west had advanced as far as the other side of these ranges. Seventeen centuries before the kings of Persia had come with their mailed cavalry toward the east, to the Indus and Samarkand—within sight of the bulwarks of the *Taghdumbash*. Two centuries later the reckless Alexander had advanced with his phalanx exactly as far.

So these ranges formed a kind of gigantic continental divide, separating the plains-dwellers of Genghis Khan from the valley-dwellers of the west, which was called by the Cathayans *Ta-tsin*, the Far Country. A gifted Cathayan general had once led an army up into these solitudes, but until now no army had ventured to make war beyond the ranges.

Now Chepé Noyon, the most impetuous of the Mongol Orkhons, had quartered himself in the heart of these ranges. And Juchi had wandered toward the setting sun into the steppe region of the Kipchak tribes. They had reported two roads through the mountain chains.

For the moment Genghis Khan was interested in trade. The goods and especially the weapons of the Mohammedan peoples beyond the rampart of mid-Asia were a great luxury to the simple-living Mongols. He encouraged his own merchants—subject Moham-medans—to send their caravans to the west.

He learned that his nearest neighbour to the west was the Shah of Kharesm, himself conqueror of a wide domain. To this Shah the Khan sent envoys, and a message.

" I send thee greeting. I know thy power and the great extent of thine empire, and I look upon thee as a most cherished son. On thy part, thou must know that I have conquered Cathay and many Turkish nations. My country is an encampment of warriors, a mine of silver, and I have no need of other lands. To me it seems that we have an equal interest in encouraging trade between our subjects."

For a Mongol of that day, this was a mild message. To the dead Emperor of Cathay, Genghis Khan had sent sheer, provocative insult. To Ala-eddin Mohammed, Shah of Kharesm, he forwarded a matter-of-fact invitation to trade. There was, to be sure, disparagement in calling the Shah his son—which in Asia implies a dependant. And there was a barb in the mention of the conquered Turkish clans. The Shah was a Turk.

The envoys of the Khan brought rich gifts to the Shah, bars of silver, precious jade and white camel's hair robes. But the barb rankled. " Who is Genghis Khan ? " he demanded. " Has he really conquered China ? "

The envoys replied that this was so.

" Are his armies as great as mine ? " the Shah then asked.

To this the envoys made response tactfully—they were Mohammedans, not Mongols—that the host of the Khan was not to be compared to his own. The Shah was satisfied, and agreed to the mutual intercourse

of merchants. Matters went well enough for a year
or so.

Meanwhile the name of Genghis Khan became
known in other Mohammedan lands. The Kalif of
Baghdad was then being oppressed by this same Shah
of Kharesm. And the Kalif was persuaded that his
cause might be aided by the shadowy Khan on the
borderland of Cathay. An envoy was sent from
Baghdad to Karakorum, and since he must pass through
the lands of the Shah to get there, certain precautions
were taken.

The chronicle has it that the authorization of this
envoy was written on his skull with a fire pencil after
his hair was shaved off. The hair was then allowed to
grow, and the envoy given his message of appeal to
study until he had it by heart. All went well. The
agent of the Kalif reached the Mongol Khan, his skull
was shaved again, his identity established and his
message repeated.

Genghis Khan paid no attention to it. In all
probability the solitary emissary and the furtive
appeal did not impress him favourably. Besides, there
was the trade agreement with the Shah.

But the Mongol's experiment with trade came to
an abrupt end. A caravan of several hundred merchants from Karakorum was seized by one, Inaljuk,
governor of Otrar, a frontier citadel belonging to the
Shah. Inaljuk reported to his master that spies were
among the merchants—which may very well have
been the case.

Mohammed Shah, without considering the matter
overmuch, sent to his governor an order to slay the
merchants, and all of them, accordingly, were put to

death. This, in due time, was reported to Genghis Khan who dispatched envoys at once to the Shah to protest. And Mohammed saw fit to slay the chief of the envoys and burn off the beards of the others.

When the survivors of his embassy returned to Genghis Khan, the master of the Gobi went apart to a mountain to meditate upon the matter. The slaying of a Mongol envoy could not go unpunished; tradition required revenge for the wrong inflicted.

"There cannot be two suns in the heavens," the Khan said, "or two *Kha Khans* upon the earth."

Then spies were sent in earnest through the mountain ranges, and couriers whipped over the desert to summon men to the standards of the horde. A brief and ominous message went this time to the Shah.

"Thou hast chosen war. That will happen which will happen, and what it is to be, we know not. God alone knows."

War, inevitable in any case between these two conquerors, had begun. And the careful Mongol had his *casus belli*.

To understand what lay before him, we must look beyond the ranges, where lay the world of Islam and the Shah.

It was a martial world, appreciative of song, with an ear not unmusical. A world beset by inward throes, slave-ridden, wealth gathering, and more than a little addicted to vice and intrigue. It left the management of its affairs to extortioners and its women to the custody of eunuchs, and its conscience to the keeping of Allah.

It followed various dogmas, and it interpreted the Koran in different ways. It gave alms to beggars, washed scrupulously, gathered in sunlit courtyards to gossip, and lived largely by favour of the great. At least once during its lifetime it made the journey to the black meteorolite under a velvet curtain within Mecca, the stone that was the Ka'aba. Upon this pilgrimage the men of Islam rubbed shoulders, renewed their zeal, and came home rather awed by the immensity of their lands and the multitudes of the believers.

Centuries ago their prophet had lighted a fire that had been carried far by the Arabs. Since then all the various peoples of Islam had been united in a common cause—conquest. The first waves of warriors had spread to Granada in Spain, and all northern Africa, Sicily and Egypt. In time the military power of Islam had passed from the Arabs to the Turks, but both had joined in the holy war against the mailed host of Christian crusaders that came to wrest Jerusalem from them.

Now in the beginning of the thirteenth century Islam was at the height of its martial power. The weakening crusaders had been driven to the coast of the Holy Land, and the first wave of the Turks was taking Asia Minor away from the soldiery of the degenerate Greek empire.

In Baghdad and Damascus the Kalifs—heads of Islam—maintained all the splendour of the days of Haroun al Rashīd and the Barmecides. Poetry and song were fine arts ; a witty saying was the making of a man. A certain observant astronomer, Omar al Khayyam, remarked that men who believed that the

pages of the Koran held all earthly lore looked more
often upon the engraving at the bottom of a bowl.

Even the reflective Omar could not ignore the
splendid pageantry of martial Islam—

" How Sultan after Sultan with his pomp
    Abode his destined hour and went his way."

The courts of Jamshid, the golden throne of
Mahmoud—Omar, penning his disconsolate quatrains,
paused to wonder at them, and to speculate upon
the possibilities of the paradise that awaited these
paladins of Islam.

Both Omar and Haroun had been for some time in
their graves, but the descendants of Mahmoud of
Ghazna ruled northern India. The Kalifs of Baghdad
had grown rather worldly wise, indulging in politics
rather than conquest. But the chivalry of Islam—that
could forget its inward quarrels and unite against an
enemy of the faith—was no less resplendent and high-
hearted than in the days when Haroun had jested with
his cup-companions.

They lived, these scions of warlike princes, in a
fertile world, where rivers flowing down from forested
ranges made the sand and clay of desert beds give
forth abundantly of grain and fruit. A warm sun
quickened intellect, and a desire for luxury. Their
weapons were fashioned by skilled armourers—steel
blades that could be bent double, shields gleaming
with silver work. They wore chain mail and light
steel helmets. They rode blooded horses, swift of
foot but not too long enduring. And the secrets of
flaming naphtha and the terrible Greek fire were
known to them.

Their life had many diversions :

" Verse and song and minstrelsy, and wine full flowing
    and sweet.
" Backgammon and chess and the hunting ground, and
    the falcon and cheetah fleet.
" Field and ball, and audience hall, and battle and banquet
    rare.
" Horse and arms and a generous hand and praise of my
    lord and prayer." *

In the centre of Islam, Mohammed Shah of
Kharesm had enthroned himself as war lord.   His
domain extended from India to Baghdad, and from the
sea of Aral to the Persian Gulf.   Except for the
Seljuk Turks, victors over the crusaders, and the
rising Mamluk dynasty in Egypt, his authority was
supreme.   He was the emperor, and the Kalif—who
quarrelled with him but might not deny him—was
restricted to the spiritual authority of a pope.

Mohammed Shah of the Kharesmian empire *†
came, like Genghis Khan, from a nomad people.   His
ancestors had been slaves, cup-bearers to the great
Seljuk Malik Shah.   He and his *atabegs* or father-
chieftains, were Turks.   A true warrior of Turan, he
had something of military genius, a grasp of things
political and no end of avarice.

We know that he indulged too much in cruelty,
putting his followers to death to gratify impulses.   He
could slay a venerable *sayyid*, and then demand
absolution from the Kalif.   Failing in this, he could
denounce the Kalif and set up another.   Hence the

* From A Literary History of Persia, by Edward G. Browne.
*† Kharesm hardly appears in the pages of history.   Like Kara K'itai
and the empire of the Chin, it was blotted out by the Mongols before it reached
the full scope of its power.

dispute that led to the sending of an envoy to Genghis Khan from Baghdad.

Then, too, Mohammed had his share of ambition and love of praise. He liked to be called the Warrior, and his courtiers extolled him as a second Alexander. He matched his mother's intrigues with oppression, and wrangled with the *wazir* who administered his affairs.

The core of his host of four hundred thousand warriors was made up of the Kharesm Turks, but he had besides the armies of the Persians at his summons. War elephants, vast camel trains, and a multitude of armed slaves followed him.

But the main defence of his empire was the chain of great cities along the rivers, Bokhara the centre of Islam's academies and mosques, Samarkand of the lofty walls and pleasure gardens, Balkh, and Herat, the heart of Khorassan.

This world of Islam, with its ambitious Shah, its multitudes of warriors and its mighty cities, was almost unknown to Genghis Khan.

CHAPTER XIII

TWO problems had to be solved before Genghis Khan could lead his army against the Mohammedan Turks. When he had moved to the conquest of China he had taken most of his desert confederacy with him. Now he must leave a vast empire behind him for several years—an empire newly knit, which must be governed even from the other side of the mountain ranges.

With this problem he dealt in his own way. Muhuli was keeping Cathay occupied with fire and sword, and the princes of Liao were busy enough restoring order behind him. Genghis Khan combed over the rest of his empire for notables in the conquered countries, men of family and ambition who might cause trouble in his absence. To each of these a Mongol courier was sent with a silver tablet and a summons to the horde. On the pretence of needing their services the Khan took them with him out of the empire.

The government itself he proposed to keep in his own hands wherever he went. He would communicate by messenger with the council of the khans in the Gobi. One of his brothers he left as governor in Karakorum.

This accomplished, there remained the second and greater problem—to transport the horde of a quarter-million warriors from Lake Baïkul over the ranges of mid-Asia into Persia. A distance of some two thousand miles as the crow flies, and a country wherein travellers to-day only venture with a well-equipped caravan. A march impossible for a modern army of that size.

He had no doubt of the ability of the horde to make the march. In it, he had fashioned a fighting force that was able to go anywhere on land. Half of it never saw the Gobi again, but some of his Mongols marched over ninety degrees of longitude and back again.

In the spring of 1219, he gave orders for the horde to rendezvous in the pasture lands of a river in the south-west. Here assembled the *tumans* under the different marshals, each man bringing with him a string of four or five horses. Great herds of cattle were driven to the pastures, and fattened comfortably during the summer. The youngest son of the Khan arrived to assume command, and in the first crisp days of autumn the Khan himself rode over from Karakorum.

He had spoken a word to the women of the nomad empire : " Ye may not bear arms, yet there is a duty for ye. Keep well the *yurts*, against the return of the men, so that the couriers and the travelling *noyons* may have a clean place and food when they halt at night. A wife may thus do honour to a warrior."

Apparently it struck him during this ride to his host that he himself might not return alive. Passing through a fine woodland, and looking at a lofty grove of pines, he remarked :

" A good place for roe-deer, and for hunting. A good resting place for an old man."

He gave orders that upon his death the *Yassa*, his code of laws, was to be read aloud, and men were to live according to it. For the horde and his officers he had other words :

" Ye go with me, to strike with our strength the man who has treated us with scorn. Ye shall share in my victories. Let the leader of ten be as vigilant and obedient as the leader of ten thousand. If either fail in duty, he will be deprived of life, and his women and children also."

After a conference with his sons and Orkhons and the various chieftains, the Khan rode out to review the different camps of the horde. He was fifty-six years old, his broad face lined, the skin hardened. He sat, his knees hunched up in the short stirrups, in the high peaked saddle of a swift-footed white charger.

In his up-tilted white felt hat were eagle feathers, and red cloth streamers hung down before either ear— like the horns of a beast, but serviceable otherwise to bind on the hat in a high wind. His long-sleeved black sable coat was bound with a girdle of gold plates or cloth of gold. He rode down the lines of the assembled squadrons, saying little. The horde was better equipped than ever before. The shock divisions had their horses encased in lacquered leather—red or black. Every man had two bows, and a spare arrow case covered to protect it against dampness. Their helmets were light and serviceable, with a leather drop, iron-studded, to guard the neck behind.

Only the regiment of the Khan's guard had shields. Besides the sabre, the men of the heavy cavalry had axes hanging from their belts, and a length of rope— lariats, or cords for pulling siege engines and bogged-down carts. Kits were small and strictly serviceable—leather sacks holding nose-bags for the pony and a pot for the man ; wax, and files for sharpening the arrow-heads, and spare bow-strings. Later on, every man would have his emergency rations—smoke-cured meat, and dry milk curds. This dried milk could be put into water and heated.

At present they were merely route marching. Many Cathayans were with them, and a new division. Apparently it was of ten thousand men, and its officer was a Cathayan, the *Ko pao yu* or Master of Artillery, and his men were skilled in building and working the heavy siege engines, the ballista, mangonels and fire throwers. These machines, it seems, were not carried entire, but their parts were stowed in the wagons. As to the *ho-pao*, the fire-gun, we shall see it in action later.*

Slowly, the horde moved through the smaller ranges, driving the cattle herds. It was about two hundred thousand strong—too great a number to keep together, as they must live on the herds and the country. Juchi, the eldest son, was detached with a couple of *tumans*, to join Chepé Noyon on the other side of the T'ian shan. The rest spread out, keeping to the valleys.

Early in the march an incident filled the astrologers with misgivings. Snow fell before its proper time. The Khan sent for Ye Liu Chutsai and demanded the meaning of the portent.

" It signifies," replied the astute Cathayan, " that the lord of the cold and wintry lands will overcome the lord of the warm climates."

* See Note VI, The Mongols and Gunpowder, page 224.

The Cathayans must have suffered that winter. Among them were men skilled in brewing herbs to cure sickness, and when a lance, stuck with its point in the ground before a tent, showed that a Mongol was sick within, these savants of herbs and stars were called upon for a remedy. Many other non-combatants kept them company—interpreters, merchants to act as spies later, mandarins to take over the administration of captured districts. Nothing was overlooked, and every detail had to be kept in order. Even lost articles had to be cared for—an officer had been appointed for this.

Metal work on the armour and saddles must be kept polished, and kits filled. The march began when the dawn drum-roll sounded, the herds being started off first, and the warriors following with the carts. At evening, the herds would be overtaken, the standard of the officer commanding pitched, and the camp would rise around it, the warriors taking their *yurts* from the camels or carts.

Rivers had to be crossed. The horses, roped together, by the saddle horns, twenty or more in a line, breasted the current. Sometimes the riders had to swim, holding to the tails. A branch would be thrust into the leather kit, and the lacing tightened, so it would float, tied to the warrior's girdle. Before long they could cross rivers on the ice.

Snow covered everything, even the sand dunes of the wastes. Withered grey tamarisk danced under the wind gusts, like the ghosts of old men. The trails were marked by antelopes' or wild sheep's horns projecting through the drifts.

Juchi's division of the horde tended off to the south,

dropping from seven-thousand foot passes into the
Pe lu, the Great North Road, above the T'ian shan.
Here, on one of the oldest trade routes of Asia, they
encountered lines of shaggy camels, bound nose-cord
to tail, plodding along to the chiming of rusty bells—
hundreds of them laden with cloth or rice or what-not,
following half a dozen men and a dog.

The main body of the horde moved more slowly
westward, dropping through gorges, and over frozen
lakes to the icy floor of the Sungarian gate, the pass
from which all the nomad clans have come out of high
Asia. Here they were buffeted by winds and chilled
by a cold so great that whole herds might be frozen if
caught in the pass during a *buran,* a black wind storm.
By now most of the cattle had died off and had been
eaten. The last stores of hay had vanished ; the carts,
perforce, had been left behind, and only the hardiest
of the camels survived.

" Even in the middle of summer," the Cathayan
Ye Liu Chutsai wrote, of the westward march,
" masses of ice and snow accumulate in these mountains. The army passing that road was obliged to
cut its way through the ice. The pines and larch trees
are so large that they seem to reach heaven. The
rivers west of the *Chin shan* (Golden mountains) all
run to the west."

To protect them, the hoofs of the unshod ponies
were bound up in strips of yak skins. The horses
seemed to suffer from the lack of fodder, and began
to bleed at the veins.

Entering the western ranges beyond the Gate of
the Winds, the warriors cut down trees, hewing out
massive timbers to be used in bridging the gorges.

The ponies dug up moss and dry grass with their hoofs
from under the snow. The hunters went afield for
game. Forging ahead in the utter cold of high Asia,
a quarter-million men endured hardships that would
have put a modern division into hospital. The Mongols
did not mind it particularly. Wrapped up in their
sheepskins and leather, they could sleep under drifting
snow ; at need, the round, heavy *yurts* warmed them.
When food failed, they opened a vein in a horse,
drank a small quantity of blood and closed the vein.

On they went, scattered over a hundred miles of
mountain country, the sledges rolling in their wake,
the bones of dead animals marking their trail.

Before the snow melted they were out on the western
steppes, riding more swiftly around bleak Lake Bal-
kash. By the time the first grass showed, they were
threading into the last barrier of the Kara Tau, the
Black Range. On lean horses, they finished the first
twelve hundred miles of their march.

Now the various divisions closed up, liaison officers
began to gallop back and forth between the commands ; the nondescript-looking merchants rode off
in groups of two or three to hunt for information. A
screen of scouts was thrown ahead of each column.

Men overhauled their kits, counted arrows, laughed
and gathered around the fires where the minstrels
knelt, droning their chants of departed heroes and
strange magic.

Through the forests, they could see below them the
first frontier of Islam, the wide river Syr, now swollen
by spring freshets.

CHAPTER XIV

THE FIRST CAMPAIGN

MEANWHILE Juchi and Chepé Noyon had had a pitched battle with the Mohammedans under the Roof of the World. It is worth telling about.

The Mohammedan Shah was in the field before the Mongols. Fresh from victories in India, he had mustered his host of four hundred thousand. He had gathered his *atabegs*, and strengthened his Turks with contingents of Arabs and Persians. This host he had led north, searching for the Mongols who were not yet on the scene. He met and attacked some of Chepé Noyon's patrols who were not aware of the war, and the appearance of these fur-clad nomads on their shaggy ponies aroused the contempt of the much better clad Kharesmians. When his spies brought him accounts of the horde, the Shah did not alter his opinion. " They have conquered only unbelievers— now the banners of Islam are arrayed against them."

Soon the Mongols were visible. Raiding detachments descended the heights toward the wide river Syr. They appeared at villages in fertile valleys, driving off the herds, gathering up all available grain and foodstuffs ; they set fire to the dwellings and retired in the smoke. Their carts and herds were sent back to the north with detachments of warriors and a day later they rode into a village fifty miles away.

These were the advance foragers, collecting supplies for the main army. There was no telling where they came from, or whither they went. They had been sent out by Juchi who was approaching through a long valley chain from the east, on the *Pe Lu*. Having an easier route than the main body of the horde, he was passing through the last ranges a little in advance of his father's horde.

Mohammed Shah left the bulk of his host at the Syr and pushed up the river toward its head-waters, working east through the ranges. Whether he learned of Juchi's advance from his scouts, or stumbled against this Mongol division by accident, he encountered it squarely in that long valley hemmed in by the forested bulwarks of the mountains.

His army was several times the strength of the Mongol division, and Mohammed—beholding for the first time the dark mass of fur and leather clad warriors without shields or chain mail—thought only of launching his attack before the strange horsemen could escape.

His disciplined Turks mustered in battle formation, and the long trumpets and cymbals sounded.

Meanwhile the Mongol general with Juchi advised the Mongol prince to retire at once and try to draw the Turks after him toward the main body of the horde. But the eldest son of the Khan gave the order to charge the Mohammedans. "If I flee, what then shall I say to my father?"

He was in command of the division, and when the order had been given the Mongols got them to horse without protest. Genghis Khan would never have suffered himself to be caught thus in the valley, or—

being caught—would have drawn back until the array of the Shah had scattered in pursuit of him. But the headstrong Juchi shot his men forward, the suicide squad* first in the advance, the heavy shock cavalry following, swords in the rein hands and long lances in the right hands. The lighter squadrons covered his flanks.

Being thus launched forward, without room for manœuvring, or time for their favourite play of arrows, the Mongol horsemen drove in grimly, using their heavier, slightly curved swords against the scimitars of the Turks.

The chronicle relates that the losses of the Mohammedans were beyond all counting, and as the Mongol advance penetrated within the centre of the Turks, the Shah himself was in danger. He saw within arrow flight the horned standards of the horde, and only the desperate efforts of his household divisions saved him from death. And Juchi's life was saved, so the story runs, by a Cathayan prince who was serving in his command.

Meanwhile the Mongol flanks had been driven in, and Jelal ed-Din, the favourite of the Kharesmian army, the eldest son of the Shah—a true Turk, small and slender and dark, loving only hard drinking and sword-play—drove home a counter charge that forced back the standards of the Mongols. The hosts of horsemen separated, at the end of the day, and during the night the Mongols played one of their customary tricks. They either set fire to the grass in the valley, or kept their own camp fires burning high as long as darkness lasted. Meanwhile Juchi and his

* The *Mangudai*, or "God-belonging" squadron, pre-doomed.

men had withdrawn, mounting fresh horses and making a march of two days in that night.

Sunrise found Mohammed and his battered squadrons occupying a valley filled with the bodies of the slain. The Mongols had vanished.

A ride over the battlefield filled the hitherto victorious Turks with misgivings. The chronicle says they lost 160,000 men in this first battle—a number certainly exaggerated, but evidence of the effect of the Mongol impact upon them—and Mohammedan warriors were always influenced by success or failure at the commencement of a campaign. Upon the Shah himself the influence of the terrible struggle in the valley was no less great. "A fear of these unbelievers was planted in the heart of the Sultan, and an estimation of their courage. If anyone spoke of them before him, he said that he had never seen men as daring and as steadfast in the throes of battle, or as skilled in giving blows with the point and edge of their swords."

No longer did the Shah think of searching for the horde in the high valleys. The country, arid in any case, had been combed over by the Mongol foragers, and could not support an army as large as his. But more than this, his dread of the strange foemen impelled him to turn back to his fortified towns along the river Syr. He sent south for reinforcements, especially for bowmen. He announced that he had won a complete victory, and in token thereof distributed robes of honour among the officers who had attended him.

Genghis Khan listened to a courier's report of the first conflict. He praised Juchi—and sent him a

supporting force of five thousand, with instructions to
follow after Mohammed.

The Mongols of Juchi—the detached left wing of
the horde—were riding through one of the garden
spots of high Asia, where every stream had its white
walled village and watch-tower. Here grew melons
and strange fruits ; the slender towers of minarets
uprose in growths of willows and poplars. To right
and left were mellow foothills, with cattle grazing on
the slopes. Behind them, the white summits of the
higher ranges reared against the sky.

" Kudjan (Khokand) abounds in pomegranates,"
the observant Ye Liu Chutsai noted down in his
geography of the journey. " They are as large as
two fists and of a sour-sweet taste. People take the
fruit and press out the juice into a vessel—a delicious
beverage for slaking thirst. Their water-melons
weigh fifty pounds, and two are a load for a
donkey."

After the winter in the frozen passes, this was luxury
indeed for the Mongol horsemen. The river widened,
and they came upon a large walled city, Khojend.
Here the supporting division of five thousand awaited
them, while laying siege to Khojend.

The commander of the Turks in the city was a
man of valour, Timur Malik, the Iron Lord. He had
withdrawn to an island with a thousand picked men
and had dug himself in. Events took a peculiar turn.

Here the river was wide, the island fortified. Timur
Malik had taken with him all available boats ; there
were no bridges. The Mongols had orders not to
leave a fortified city behind them. And they could

CHAPTER XV

BOKHARA

WHEN the Shah rode down from the higher ranges, he turned north toward the Syr with his host, waiting for the arrival of the horde itself, intending to give battle when it attempted to cross the river. But he waited in vain.

To appreciate what happened now we must glance at the map. This northern portion of Mohammed's empire was half fertile valley land, half arid and sandy plains, cut up into strata of red clay, dust-covered and lifeless. So the cities existed only along the rivers and within the hills.

Two mighty rivers flowed north-west across this desert floor, to empty their waters six hundred miles away into the salt sea of Aral. The first of these rivers was the Syr, the Jaxartes of the ancients. And here were walled cities joined by caravan roads—a kind of chain of human life and dwellings extending through the barrens. The second river, to the south, was the Amu, once called the Oxus. And near this stood the citadels of Islam, Bokhara and Samarkand.

The Shah was encamped behind the Syr, unable to learn whither the Mongols were moving. He expected fresh armies from the south and the revenues of a new tax levy. This mobilization was interrupted by alarming news. Mongols had been seen descending from the high passes two hundred miles to his right, and almost in his rear.

What had happened was that Chepé Noyon, leaving Juchi, had crossed the mountains to the south—had stolen up on the Turkish contingents that were watching this route into Kharesm, and was now marching swiftly around the glaciers of the Amu head-waters. And, not more than a couple of hundred miles distant, Samarkand lay in his path. Chepé Noyon had no more than twenty thousand men with him, but the Shah could not know this.

Mohammed, instead of being reinforced, was now in a fair way to be cut off from his second and main line of defence, the Amu with its great cities, Bokhara and Samarkand. Aroused by the new danger, Mohammed did something for which he has been severely criticized by Mohammedan chroniclers in later years. He split up half his host among the fortified cities.

Some 40,000 were sent to strengthen the garrisons along the Syr, and he marched south with the bulk of his forces, detaching 30,000 toward Bokhara, and leading the rest to Samarkand, the menaced point. He did this, assuming that the Mongols would not be able to storm his citadels, and would retire after a season of raiding and plundering. He was mistaken in both surmises.

Even before this two sons of the Khan had appeared at Otrar, down the Syr to the north. Otrar, whose governor had put to death Mongol merchants. Inaljuk, who had ordered the execution of the merchants, was still governor of the city. Knowing that he had little mercy to expect from the Mongols, he shut himself up in the citadel with the best of his men,

and held out for five months. He fought to the end,
taking refuge in a tower when the Mongols had cut
down or captured the last of his men ; and when his
arrows gave out, he still hurled stones down on his
foes. Taken alive, in spite of this desperation, he was
sent to the Khan, who ordered molten silver to be
poured into his eyes and ears—the death of retri-
bution. The walls of Otrar were razed and all its
people driven away.

While this was going on, a second Mongol army
approached the Syr and took Tashkent. A third
detachment scoured the northern end of the Syr,
storming the smaller towns. The Turkish garrison
abandoned Jend, and the townspeople surrendered
when the Mongols planted their ladders and swarmed
along the walls. In such cases in this first year of the
war, the warriors of the Shah, the Turkish garrisons,
were massacred by the Mongols, the townspeople—
who were native Persians for the most part—driven
out of the city, which was then plundered at leisure.

Then the captives would be sorted out, the strong
young men kept to labour at siege work in the next
city, the artisans to do skilled work for the conquerors.
In one case, where a Mohammedan merchant, an
envoy of the Mongols, had been torn to pieces by the
men of a town, the terrible Mongol storm was begun
—the attack that is never allowed to cease, fresh
warriors taking the place of the slain, until the place
was carried and its people slain with the sword or
arrows.

Genghis Khan did not appear at all along the Syr.
He vanished from sight, taking the centre of the horde
with him. No one knows where he crossed the river,

or where he went. But he must have made a wide circle through the Red Sands desert, because he appeared out of the barrens, marching swiftly on Bokhara *from the west*.

Mohammed was not merely outflanked. He was in danger of being cut off from his southern armies, his son and reinforcements and the rich lands of Khorassan and Persia. While Chepé Noyon was advancing from the east, Genghis Khan was moving in from the west, and the Shah at Samarkand might well feel that the jaws of a trap were closing in on him.

In this predicament, he divided his main army between Bokhara and Samarkand, sending other of his *atabegs* to Balkh and Kunduz. With no more than his own attendant nobles, his elephants and camels and household troops, he left Samarkand. And he took with him his treasure and his family, intending to return at the head of a fresh army.

In this expectation, also, he was disappointed.

Mohammed, the Warrior, called by his people a second Alexander, had been thoroughly outgeneralled. The Mongols under the sons of the Khan, carrying fire and sword along the Syr, had been no more than so many masks for the real attacks thrust home by Chepé Noyon and Genghis Khan.

The Khan hastened out of the desert—so eager to make haste that he did not linger to molest the little towns in his path, and asked only water for his horses. He expected to surprise Mohammed at Bokhara ; but when he arrived he learned that the Shah had fled. He was confronted by one of the strongholds of Islam, the city of academies, by a wall twelve leagues—so says the chronicle—in circuit, through which ran a fair river, lined with gardens and pleasure houses. It was garrisoned by some 20,000 Turks and a multitude of Persians, and honoured by many an *imam* and *sayyid*, the savants of Islam, the interpreters of the Book to be Read.

It had within it a latent fire, the zeal of the devout Mohammedans, who were at present in a very mixed frame of mind. The wall was too strong to be carried by assault, and if the mass of the inhabitants had chosen to defend it, months might have passed before the Mongols could have won a foothold upon it.

Genghis Khan had said with much truth, " The strength of a wall is neither greater nor less than the courage of the men who defend it." In this case, the Turkish officers chose to leave the townspeople to their fate and escape to join the Shah. So they went out, with the soldiery of the Shah at night, by the water gate, and headed toward the Amu.

The Mongols suffered them to pass, but three *tumans* followed them and came up with them at the river. Here the Turks were attacked and nearly all of them put to the sword.

Abandoned by the garrison, the elders of the city, the judges and *imams*, consulted together and went out to face the strange Khan, yielding him the keys of the city, and receiving his promise that the lives of the inhabitants should be spared. The governor with the remaining warriors shut himself up in the citadel, which was at once beset by the Mongols, who shot flaming arrows into the place until the roofs of the palaces caught fire.

A flood of horsemen filled the wide streets of the

city, breaking into the granaries and storehouses, stabling their horses in the libraries, to the frantic sorrow of the Mohammedans who beheld more than once the sacred leaves of the Koran trodden under the hoofs of the ponies. The Khan himself drew rein before an imposing building, the great mosque of the city, and asked if it were the house of the emperor. He was told that it was the house of Allah.

At once he rode his horse up the steps and into the mosque, dismounting, and ascending to the reader's desk with its giant Koran. Here, in his black lacquer armour and leather-curtained helmet, he addressed the assembled mullahs and scholars, who had expected to behold fire descend from Heaven to blast this ungainly figure in strange armour.

"I have come to this place," he said to them, " only to tell you that you must find provender for my army. The countryside is bare of hay and grain, and my men are suffering from want. Open, then, the doors of your storehouses."*

But when the Mohammedan elders hastened from the mosque they found the warriors of the Gobi already installed in the granaries, and the horses stabled. This portion of the horde had made a forced march over the desert floor for too many days to linger upon the threshold of plenty.

From the mosque, the Khan went to the city square where orators were accustomed to assemble an audience to lecture upon matters of science or doctrine.

"Who is this man ? " demanded a newcomer, of a venerable *sayyid*.

* This passage is almost invariably misquoted in histories, and given as follows : "Genghis Khan rode into the mosque and shouted to *his men,* ' The hay is cut—give your horses fodder.' "

"Hush!" whispered the other. "It is the anger of God that descends upon us."

The Khan—a man who knew well how to address a multitude, says the chronicle—ascended the speaker's rostrum and faced the people of Bokhara. First he questioned them closely about their religion, and commented gravely that it was a mistake to make the pilgrimage to Mecca. "For the power of Heaven is not in one place alone, but in every corner of the earth."

The old chieftain, shrewd in gauging the moods of his listeners, fanned the superstitious dread of the Mohammedans. To them he appeared as a pagan devastator, an incarnation of uncouth and barbaric power, a little grotesque. Bokhara had seen none but the devout within its walls.

"The sins of your emperor are many," he assured them. "I have come—I, the wrath and the flail of Heaven, to destroy him as other emperors have been crushed. Do not give him protection or aid."

He waited for the interpreter to explain his words. The Mohammedans seemed to him to be like the Cathayans, builders of cities, makers of books. Useful in furnishing him with provisions, in yielding up their wealth—in giving him information about the rest of the world ; useful in giving labourers and slaves to his men—artisans to send back to the Gobi.

"You have done well," he went on, " in supplying my army with food. Bring now to my officers the precious things you have hidden away. Do not trouble about what is lying loose in your houses—we will take care of that."

The rich men of Bokhara were placed under guard

of Mongols who did not leave them, day or night. Some, on suspicion that they had not brought out all their concealed wealth, were tortured. The Mongol officers called for dancing girls and musicians to play Mohammedan pieces. Sitting gravely, wine cup in hand, in the mosques and palaces, they watched this spectacle of the entertainment of the people who lived in cities and gardens.

The garrison in the citadel held out bravely and inflicted losses that angered the Mongols before the governor and his followers were cut down. When the last valuables had been retrieved from cellars and wells and dug up from the earth, the inhabitants were driven out into the plain. The Mohammedan chronicler gives us a clear glimpse of the misery of his people.

"It was a fearful day. One heard only the weeping of men, women and children, who were to be separated for ever; women were ravished by the barbarians under the eyes of those who had no resource save sorrow; some of the men, rather than witness the shame of their families, rushed upon the warriors and died fighting."

Different parts of the city were fired, and the flames swept through the dry structures of wood and baked clay, a pall of smoke rising over Bokhara, hiding the sun. The captives were driven toward Samarkand, and, unable to keep up with the mounted Mongols, suffered terribly during the brief march.

Genghis Khan only stayed two hours in Bokhara, hastening on to seek the Shah in Samarkand. On the way he was met by the detachments of the horde from the Syr, and his sons gave him the tidings of the capture of the cities along the northern line.

Samarkand was the strongest of the Shah's cities. He had started building a new wall, massive in size, about the circuit of its gardens. But the swift advance of the Mongols found the new rampart unfinished. The old defences were formidable enough, including twelve iron gates flanked by towers. Twenty armoured elephants and one hundred and ten thousand warriors, Turks and Persians, had been left to guard it. The Mongols were less numerous than the garrison, and Genghis Khan made preparations for a long siege— assembling the people of the countryside and the captives from Bokhara to aid in the work.

If the Shah had remained with his men, or if an officer like Timur Malik had been in command, Samarkand might well have held out as long as food lasted. But the swift and methodical preparations of the Mongols alarmed the Mohammedans, who beheld in the distance the vast multitude of captives, and thought the horde much greater than it was. The garrison sallied out once—was drawn on into one of the usual Mongol ambushes—and fared badly. The losses in this battle disheartened the defenders and the *imams* and judges went out, on the morning the Mongols were preparing to storm one portion of the wall, and surrendered the city. Thirty thousand Kankali Turks on their own account went over to the Mongols—were received amiably, given Mongol military dress and massacred a night or two later. The Mongols would never trust the Turks of Kharesm, especially those who turned traitor.

When the skilled labourers of the city had been

led out to the horde and able-bodied men picked for other work, the rest of the inhabitants were suffered to go back to their houses. But a year or so later they were summoned to the horde.

Ye Liu Chutsai writes of Samarkand, " Around the city to an extent of several scores of miles there are everywhere orchards, groves, flower gardens, aqueducts, running springs, square basins and round ponds in uninterrupted succession. Indeed, Samarkand is a delicious place."

CHAPTER XVI

A T Samarkand it was reported to Genghis Khan that Mohammed Shah had forsaken the city and gone south. The Mongol was determined to make the Shah captive before new armies could be raised against the invaders. He had failed to come up with the monarch of Kharesm, and now he sent for Chepé Noyon and Subotai and gave them orders.

"Follow Mohammed Shah wherever he goes in the world. Find him, alive or dead. Spare the cities that open their gates to you but take by assault those that resist. I think you will not find this as difficult as it seems."

A strange task, to hunt down an emperor through a dozen kingdoms. It was a task, indeed, for the most reckless and the most infallible of the Orkhons. They were given two *tumans*, twenty thousand men. With these instructions and with this cavalry division, the two Orkhons set out at once toward the south. It was then April, 1220, the Year of the Serpent.

Mohammed had gone south from Samarkand to Balkh, on the edge of the lofty ranges of Afghanistan. As usual, he vacillated. Jelal ed-Din was far off in the north, raising a new army among the warriors of the desert country near the sea of Aral. But Genghis

146

Khan, at Bokhara, was between the Shah and this possible rallying point.

He thought of entering the Afghan country, where warlike clans awaited him. Finally, hesitating between varied counsel and his own dread, he turned due west, crossing the barrens to the mountain region of northern Persia, and arrived at Nisapur, putting, as he thought, five hundred miles between him and the Mongol horde.

Chepé Noyon and Subotai found a strong city barring the passage of the Amu ; they swam their horses across, and learned from scouts in the advance that Mohammed had forsaken Balkh. So they turned west, into the barrens, separating for greater protection and to obtain all possible grazing for their horses.

Every man of the two picked *tumans* had several horses, in good condition, and the grass along the scattered streams and wells was fresh. They must have covered eighty miles a day, changing to untired horses several times during the day, and dismounting only at sunset to eat cooked food. At the end of the barrens they encountered the rose gardens and white walls of ancient Merv.

Satisfying themselves that the Shah could not be in this city, they galloped down to Nisapur, coming in three weeks after Mohammed—who had learned of their mission, and fled on pretence of a hunting expedition. Nisapur closed its gates and the Orkhons assaulted it furiously. They failed to carry the walls but became certain that the Shah was not within its defences.

They picked up the scent again, and headed west along the caravan route that leads to the Caspian, scattering the remnants of the Shah's armies that had chosen this way to safety from the Mongol terror. Near modern Teheran they met and defeated a Persian army, thirty thousand strong.

Again they separated—all trace of the fleeing emperor vanished for the moment—Subotai tending north through the mountain region, Chepé Noyon galloping south along the edge of the salt desert. They had passed out of Kharesm proper—had outrun the very tidings of their coming.

Mohammed, meanwhile, had sent away first his family, then his treasure. He left the caskets containing his jewels at a fortress—where the Mongols found them later—and decided to journey to Baghdad, to Baghdad where ruled the very Kalif with whom he had quarrelled in other days. He picked up men here and there, a following of a few hundred. He followed the great road that leads to Baghdad.

But at Hamadan the Mongols appeared at his heels. His men were scattered and ridden down, and a few arrows shot at him—the Mongols unaware of his identity. He escaped and doubled back toward the Caspian. Some of his Turkish warriors grew discontented and rebellious, and Mohammed saw fit to sleep in a small tent pitched beside his own. And one morning he found the empty tent filled with arrows.

" Is there no place on earth," he asked an officer, " where I can be safe from the Mongol thunderbolt ? "

He was advised to take ship on the Caspian and go out to an island where he could be hidden until his sons and *atabegs* could collect an army strong enough to defend him.

This Mohammed did. Disguising himself, with a

few nondescript followers, he passed through the gorges, seeking a small town on the western shore of the Caspian—a place of fishermen and merchants, tranquil enough. But the Shah, weary and ill, deprived of his court, his slaves and cup companions, would not sacrifice the prestige of his name. He insisted on reading the public prayers in the mosque, and his identity did not long remain a secret.

A Mohammedan, who once suffered oppression at the hand of the Shah, betrayed him to the Mongols who had scattered another Persian army at Kasvin, and were questing after Mohammed through the hills. They rode into the town that had sheltered him, as he was preparing to enter a fishing skiff.

Arrows flew, but the boat drew away from the shore and some of the nomads in their rage actually urged their horses into the water. They swam after the skiff until the strength of men and beasts gave out and they disappeared in the waves.

Although they never laid hand on the Shah, they had slain him. Weakened by disease and hardship this overlord of Islam died on his island, so poverty-ridden that his only shroud was a shirt of one of his followers.

Chepé Noyon and Subotai, the two veteran marauders who had been ordered to capture the Shah alive or dead, did not know that he lay buried on his barren island—another unfortunate who had fared no better than Wai Wang of Cathay, and Prester John himself, and Toukta Beg and Gutchluk. They sent back to the Khan the bulk of his treasure that the careful Subotai had gathered up, and most of his family, and word that he had sailed eastward in a ship.

Genghis Khan, believing that Mohammed would try to join his son at Urgench, the city of the Khans, sent a division in that direction.

But Subotai, wintering in the snow-bound pastures of the Caspian, conceived the idea of marching to the north, around the sea to rejoin his Khan. He sent a courier to Samarkand to ask permission to make this journey, and Genghis Khan gave his assent, sending along several thousand Turkomans to strengthen the Orkhon's force. Subotai, on his own account, had been recruiting among the wild Kurds. After going south a bit to besiege and storm the important cities they had passed by in hunting down Mohammed, the Mongols turned north, into the Caucasus.

They raided Georgia. A desperate struggle took place between the Mongols and the warriors of the mountains. Chepé Noyon hid himself on one side of the long valley that leads up to Tiflis, while Subotai made use of the old Mongol trick of pretended flight. The five thousand men in ambush sallied out upon the flank of the Georgians, who suffered terribly in the battle.*

The Mongols slashed their way through the gorges of the Caucasus, and passed the Iron Gate of Alexander. Emerging upon the northern slopes they found an army of the mountain peoples—Alans, Circassians and Kipchaks mustered against them. They were outnumbered vastly, and had no way of retreat ; but Subotai succeeded in detaching the nomad Kipchaks

* See Note VII, The Conjurers and the Cross, page 228.

from the others, and the Mongols rode through the stalwart Alans and Circassians.

Then, following the Kipchaks into the salt steppes beyond the Caspian, the marauders out of Cathay scattered these wary nomads, driving them steadily north into the lands of the Russian princes.

And here they were met by a new and utterly brave foeman. The Russian warriors gathered from Kiev and the far dukedoms, eighty-two thousand of them. They moved down the Dnieper escorted by strong bands of Kipchaks. They were sturdy horsemen, shield-bearers, who had waged from times forgotten a feud with the nomads of the steppes.

The Mongols drew back from the Dnieper for nine days, watching the Russian masses, until they reached a place selected beforehand to give battle. The northern warriors were scattered in different camps, formidable enough, but sluggish and quarrelling among themselves. They had no leader like Subotai. For two days the struggle between Russian and Mongol—their first meeting—went on in the steppe. The great prince died under the pagan's weapons, with his nobles, and few of the host lived to ascend the Dnieper again.

Left once more to their own devices, Subotai and Chepé Noyon wandered down into the Crimea and stormed a Genoese trade citadel. What next they might have done there is no knowing. They were intent on crossing the Dnieper into Europe when Genghis Khan, who had followed their movements by courier, ordered them to return to a rendezvous some two thousand miles in the east.

Chepé Noyon died on the way, but the Mongols

turned aside long enough to invade and devastate the Bulgars, who were then on the Volga.

It was an amazing march, and probably it remains to-day the greatest feat of cavalry in human annals. It could only have been accomplished by men of remarkable endurance, utterly confident in their own powers.

" Have you never heard," cries the Persian chronicler, " that a band of men from the place where the sun rises, overrode the earth to the Caspian Gates, carrying destruction among peoples and sowing death in its passage ? Then, returning to its master—it arrived sound and hale, loaded with booty. And this in less than two years."

This gallop of two divisions to the end of ninety degrees of longitude bore strange fruit. Beside the warriors rode the savants of Cathay and the Ugurs, Nestorian Christians among them. At least we hear of Mohammedan merchants with an eye for trade, who sold Christian ecclesiastical manuscripts to some of the horde.

And Subotai did not ride blindly. The Cathayans and Ugurs noted down the positions of the rivers they crossed, and of lakes that yielded fish—of salt mines and silver mines. Post stations were planted along the route—*darogas* appointed in captured districts. With the fighting Mongol came the administrative mandarin. A captive Armenian bishop—he was kept to read and write letters for them—tells us that in the lands beneath the Caucasus, a census was made of all men over the age of ten.

Subotai had discovered the vast pasture lands of southern Russia, the black earth region. He remem-

bered these steppes. Years later he returned from the
other side of the world to overrun Moscow. And he
took up his march again where he had been called
back by the Khan, crossing the Dnieper to invade
eastern Europe.*

And the Genoese and Venetian merchants were
brought into contact with the Mongols. A generation
later the Polos, of Venice, set out for the dominion of
the Grand Khan.*†

* See Note VIII, Subotai Bahadur *v.* Middle Europe, page 229.
*† See Note IX, What Europe thought of the Mongols, page 236.

CHAPTER XVII

WHILE the two Orkhons were raiding the west of the Caspian sea, two sons of the Khan journeyed to the other inland sea, now known as the Aral. They had been sent forth to gather news of the Shah and to cut off his return. Learning at length that he was in his grave, they followed the wide Amu through its clay steppes to the native city of the Kharesmians.

Here the Mongols settled down to a long and bitter siege, in which—lacking large stones for their casting machines, they hewed massive tree trunks into blocks and soaked the wood until heavy enough for their purpose. In the hand-to-hand fighting that lasted within the walls for a week, the chroniclers say they used flaming naphtha—a new weapon that they must have picked up among the Mohammedans, who had handled it with devastating effect against the crusaders of Europe. Urgench fell, and they trotted back with their captives and spoil to the headquarters of the Khan, but Jelal ed-Din, the valiant son of a weak father, escaped to lead fresh forces against them.

Meanwhile Genghis Khan withdrew his warriors from the lowlands during the heat of the summer—a burning, sultry heat that distressed the men accustomed to the high altitudes of the Gobi. He led them up into the cooler ranges beyond the Amu.

To keep them occupied while the horse herds grazed —and with an eye to discipline—he issued an order for the favourite pastime of the horde, a season's hunt.

A Mongol hunt was no less than a regular campaign, against beasts instead of men. The whole horde shared in it, and its rules had been laid down by the Khan himself, which meant that they were inexorable.

Juchi, the Master of Hunting, being absent on duty, his lieutenant galloped off to survey and mark several hundred miles of hills. Streamers were planted for the starting points of the various regiments. Beyond the horizon the *gurtai*, or closing point of the hunt, was chosen and likewise marked.

Witness then, the squadrons of the horde, in high fettle, moving off to right and left, bivouacking under the orders of the hunters, waiting the arrival of the Khan and the fanfare of horns and cymbals that would start them off. They were thus arranged in a shallow half-circle, covering perhaps eighty miles or so of countryside.

The Khan appearing with his higher officers, and princes and youthful grandsons, the riders mounted, forming a close-knit line, sometimes two ranks deep. They carried all weapons and equipment used against human enemies, with the addition of wicker shields.

The horses surged forward, the officers dropped behind their commands, and the rousing of the animals began. The warriors were forbidden to use their arms against the animals, and it was a real disgrace to allow any four-footed thing to slip through the line of riders. They crushed through thickets, beat up gullies and climbed hillocks, shouting and clamouring when a tiger or wolf was seen sliding out of the brush.

Matters went a little harder in the night. After the first month of the hunt, great numbers of animals were massing ahead of the half-circle of humans. The warriors went into camp, lighted fires, posted sentries. There was even the usual password. Officers went the rounds. No easy matter to keep a line of pickets when all the four-footed life of the mountains was astir in front of them—eyes glowing from the ground, the howling of wolves and the spitting snarl of leopards breaking through the silence.

Harder still a month later, when the circle had drawn in a little and the multitude of animals began to feel it was being driven. No relaxing the rigour of the hunt. If a fox went to earth it must be dug out again with mattocks ; if a bear trundled into a hole in the rocks, someone must go in after it—without injuring the bear ! Many a chance here for the young warriors to show their skill and fearlessness, especially if a solitary tusked boar—or a herd—turned and rushed the line of riders.

One part of the line encountered the wide bend of a river, and was held up. Straightway couriers were sent speeding along the half-circle of the hunters, with orders to hold back the rest of the line until the river could be crossed. The driven beasts were already over, for the most part.

The warriors urged in their horses, and slipped from the saddles, clinging to mane or tail. Some laced up their leather kits air-tight and used them as rude

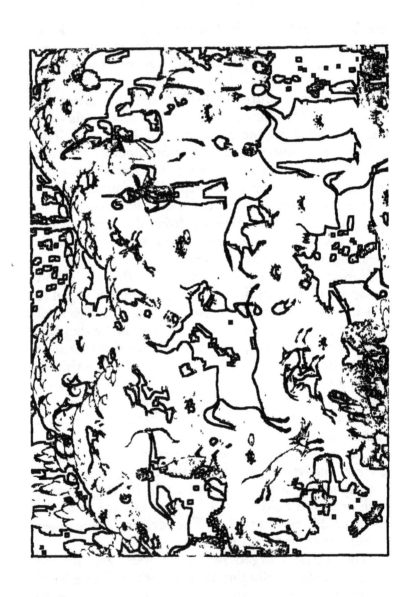

floats. Once on the far bank they mounted again, and the hunt went forward.

Here and there appeared the old Khan, watching the behaviour of the men, and the way the officers handled them. He said nothing during the hunt, but he remembered such details.

Guided by the huntsmen, the half-circle closed its wings, nearing the *gurtai*. The beasts began to feel the pressure—deer leaping into view with quivering flanks, tigers turning this way and that, heads lowered, snarling. Out of sight, beyond the *gurtai*, the circle was closed, tightening around the game. The brazen clamour of cymbals and the roar of shouting grew louder; the ranks formed two and three deep; the Khan, riding up to the mass of men and frantic beasts, gave a signal. The riders parted to let him through.

By old custom the Khan was to be first among the cornered beasts. He carried a bare sword in one hand, his bow in the other. It was permissible to use weapons now. The chroniclers say that he picked out the more dangerous of the brute antagonists, launching his arrows at a tiger, or reining his horse against wolves.

When he had killed several beasts, he withdrew from the ring, riding up a hill overlooking the *gurtai* and sitting there under a pavilion to watch the exploits of the princes and officers who next entered. It was a Mongol arena, the gladiatorial games of the nomads, and as with the gladiators of Rome not a few who entered the arena were carried from it mangled or lifeless.

When the signal for the general slaying was given, the warriors of the horde surged forward, taking what lay in their path. A whole day might pass in this slaughter of game—until the grandsons and boy princes of the horde came, as custom required, to the Khan to beg that the surviving animals should be allowed to live. This request was granted, and the hunters turned to gather up the carcases.

This hunting trained the warriors, and the closing in of the ring of riders was used in warfare against human beings as well.

In this year and in an enemy country, the hunt lasted no longer than four months. The Khan wished to be ready for the autumn campaign, and to meet Juchi and Chatagai, returning from the inland sea with word of the death of the Shah.

Until now the Mongols had marched almost without interruption through Islam. They had crossed rivers, and taken cities, as swiftly as a modern traveller with servants and a caravan might pass from place to place. Mohammed the Warrior, too ambitious in the beginning, too fearful in the end, had abandoned his people to try to save himself and had earned thereby only ignominy and a beggar's grave.

Like the emperor of Cathay, he had thrown his armies into cities to escape the Mongol cavalry that remained invisible until the hour of battle and then manœuvred in terrible silence in obedience to the signals given by moving the standards—signals that were repeated to the warriors of a squadron by the arm movements of an officer. This, during the day and in the din of conflict when the human voice could not be heard and cymbals and kettle drums might be mistaken for the enemy's instruments. At night such signals were given by the raising and lowering of

coloured lanterns near the *tugh* or standard of the
commander.

After the first rush upon the northern line of the
Syr, Genghis Khan had concentrated his columns on
what he thought to be the chief cities of the empire,
Bokhara and Samarkand. He had broken this second
line of defence without serious trouble, and had
concentrated the horde again in what might be called
the third line—the fertile hills of northern Persia and
Afghanistan.

So far the struggle between Mongol and Turk—
unbeliever and Mohammedan—had been utterly
disastrous for the latter. The Mongols appeared to the
dismayed Turks to be an incarnation of divine wrath
—in all truth, a scourge visited upon them for their
sins.

Genghis Khan was at some pains to encourage this
belief. He had also taken care to clear his flanks to
the east, riding himself through the tablelands around
the Amu head-waters, and sending other divisions to
occupy the cities in the west that Chepé Noyon and
Subotai had passed by—sending back a report of
them to the Khan. This done, he had made himself
master of Balkh and had devoted a summer to the
great hunt near by.

Here he occupied the trade routes in the centre of
the Mohammedan peoples. He had been gathering
information all this while, and he knew now that there
were forces still untouched to be dealt with, and greater
powers beyond the horizon. As the Chinese had done,
the population of Islam was arming against him.
Their Shah lost to them, and two of his sons killed in
battle against the Mongols, they began to muster

under their natural leaders, the Persian princes and the *sayyids*, the descendants of a warrior prophet.

Genghis Khan was quite aware of his situation. He knew that the real test of strength was before him—that perhaps a million men, good horsemen and exceedingly well armed, were now ready to move against him. For the present they lacked a leader and they were scattered throughout a dozen kingdoms, in a circle around him.

The horde, in the beginning of this second year, could not have numbered more than twelve *tumans*, somewhat more than a hundred thousand. The Idikut of the Ugurs and the Christian king of Almalykhad asked leave to go back to the T'ian shan with their forces, and he had given them permission to do so. His best leaders, Chepé Noyon and Subotai, were in the west, with two *tumans*. Tilik Noyon, the most dependable of his remaining Orkhons, had been killed in the assault of Nisapur. Muhuli, of course, was occupied in Cathay. The fellowship of the Orkhons had thinned, and Genghis Khan felt the need of Subotai's counsel.

So he sent for his favourite general, all the way to the Caspian. Subotai came back to Balkh in answer to the summons, and talked for a few days with the Khan, then galloped back to his headquarters a thousand miles away.

The mood of the Khan had changed and he no longer thought of hunting. He reproached his eldest son Juchi angrily for the quarrel that had delayed the capture of Urgench—or perhaps for allowing Jelal ed-Din to escape. And the wayward and defiant Juchi was sent from the horde. With his household troops, he rode north into the steppes beyond the sea of Aral.

Then Genghis Khan ordered the horde forth, no longer to manœuvre and pillage with half-indifferent contempt of their foes, but to destroy the man-power that existed around him.

CHAPTER XVIII

" I WAS living," relates the chronicle of a prince of Khorassan, " at the time in my citadel on a high and stony mountainside. It was one of the strongest of Khorassan, and—if tradition is to be believed—belonged to my ancestors since Islamism was brought into these lands. As it is near the centre of the province, it served as asylum to escaped prisoners and to inhabitants who fled from captivity or death at the hands of the Tatars.

" After some time the Tatars appeared before it. When they saw that they could not take it, they demanded as the price of their withdrawal ten thousand robes of cotton cloth, and a quantity of other things —although they were already gorged with the sack of Nesa.

" I consented to this. But when it came to carrying the ransom out to them, no one could be found to undertake it, because everyone knew that their Khan made a practice of slaying whosoever came into their hands. Finally two old men offered themselves, bringing me their children and commending them to my care if they should lose their lives. Actually, the Tatars did slay them before leaving.

" Soon these barbarians spread all through Khorassan. When they arrived in a district they drove

162

before them the peasantry, and brought the captives to the city they wished to take, using them in working the siege-engines. Fright and desolation became all-pervading. The man who had been made captive was more tranquil than the one who waited in his house, not knowing what his fate would be. Chieftains and nobles were obliged to go with their vassals and war machines. Everyone who did not obey was, without exception, put to the point of the sword."

It was Tuli, the youngest son of the Khan, Master of War, who thus invaded the fertile provinces of Persia. He had been ordered by his father to look for Jelal ed-Din, but the Kharesmian prince evaded him, and the Mongol army marched against Merv—the jewel of the sands, the pleasure city of the Shahs. It stood on the River of Birds, the *Murgh Ab*, and sheltered in its libraries many thousand volumes of manuscript.

The Mongols discovered a roving column of Turkomans in the vicinity, scattered them, and Tuli made the round of the walls with his officers, studying the defences. The Mongol lines were drawn up closer, the investment completed ; the cattle of the Turkomans were turned out to graze.

Angered by the loss of a thousand of his best men —imperial guardsmen of the Khan—Tuli launched storm after storm against the wall of Merv, building an embankment of earth against the rampart and covering his onset with flights of arrows. For twenty-two days this went on, and during the lull that followed, an *imam* was sent out to the Mongols, who received him with all courtesy and returned him safely to his lines.

This man of religion, it appears, had not come on behalf of the city itself but on behest of the governor, a certain Merik. Reassured, the governor went forth to the Mongol tents bearing with him rich gifts of silver vessels and jewelled robes.

Tuli, a master of deceit, had a robe of honour sent to Merik, and invited him to his own tent to dine. There he convinced the Persian that he would be spared.

"Summon then thy friends and chosen companions," Tuli suggested. "I will find work for them to do, and will honour them."

Merik despatched a servant to bring out his intimates, who were seated beside the governor at the feast. Tuli then asked for a list of the six hundred richest men of Merv, and the governor and his intimates obediently wrote out the names of the wealthiest landholders and merchants. Then, before the horrified Merik, his companions were strangled by the Mongols. The list of the six hundred names in the governor's handwriting was taken to the gate of Merv by one of Tuli's officers, who demanded the persons in question.

In due course, they appeared and were placed under guard. The Mongols made themselves masters of the gate, and their bands of horsemen pushed into the streets of Merv. All the inhabitants were ordered out into the plain with their families and such goods as they could carry. This evacuation lasted four days.

In the midst of the multitude of captives Tuli sat watching, from his chair on a gilded dais. His officers singled out the leaders of the Persian soldiery and brought them before him. While the others looked on, helpless, the heads were cut from the officers of Merv.

Then the men, women and children were separated into three masses—the men forced to lie down, their arms across their backs. All this unhappy multitude was divided among the Mongol warriors who strangled and slashed them to death, excepting only four hundred craftsmen who were needed by the horde, and some children to be kept as slaves. The six hundred wealthy inhabitants fared little better—being tortured until they led the Mongols to where they had hidden their most precious possessions.

The vacant dwellings were ransacked by the Mongols, the walls razed to the ground, and Tuli drew off. The only survivors of the city, apparently, were some five thousand Mohammedans who had concealed themselves in cellars and conduits, and these did not live long. Some troops of the horde returned to the city, hunted them down and left the place empty of human life.

In this fashion, one by one, sister cities were tricked and stormed. At one place some people saved themselves by lying down among the knots of bodies of those already slain. The Mongols heard of this, and an order was issued to cut the heads from the inhabitants in future. In the ruins of another city some few score of Persians managed to survive. A troop of Mongols was sent back with orders to exterminate the survivors. The nomads went into camp and tracked and hunted down the miserable people with less compunction than if they had been animals.

It was, in fact, very much like the hunting of the

animals. Every trick of ingenuity was called into play to root out human beings. In the ruins of one place the Mongols forced a captive *muezzin* to cry the summons to prayer from a minaret. The Moham-medans, lurking in their hiding places, came forth in the belief that the terrible invaders had left. They were destroyed.

When the Mongols abandoned the site of a city they trampled and burned whatever crops might be left standing so that those who escaped their swords would starve to death. At Urgench, where the long defence had made them suffer, they actually went to the trouble to dam up the river above the citadel, altering its course so it flowed over the debris of houses and walls. This changing of the course of the Amu puzzled geographers for a long time.

Such details are too horrible to dwell upon to-day. It was war carried to its utmost extent—an extent that was very nearly approached in the last European war. It was the slaughter of human beings without hatred—simply to make an end of them.

It made a *tabula rasa* of the heart of Islam. The survivors of the massacres lived on so shaken in spirit that they cared for nothing except to find food and to hide, too fearful to leave the weed-grown debris until the wolves who came to the unburied dead exterminated them or drove them away. Such sites of destroyed cities were forbidden to human beings —a scar on the face of a once fertile earth. More than once earth was ploughed into the ruins, and grain planted.

The nomads, valuing human life less than the soil that could nourish grain and beasts, were eradicating the cities. Genghis Khan had paralysed the growing movement of rebellion—had broken resistance before it could form against him. He would allow no mercy.

" I forbid you," he said to his Orkhons, " to show clemency to my enemies without an express order from me. Rigour alone keeps such spirits dutiful. An enemy conquered is not subdued, and will always hate his new master."

He had not used such measures in the Gobi, nor such utter cruelty in Cathay. Here, in the world of Islam, he showed himself a veritable scourge. He reproved Tuli bitterly for sparing the inhabitants of Herat—with the exception of ten thousand partisans of the Sultan Jelal ed-Din. And, in fact, Herat did rebel against its yoke, putting to death its Mongol governor.

Other cities flared up for a moment—when the youthful sultan visited them and harangued them. But the squadrons of the Khan were soon at their gates. The fate of Herat was not less hideous than that of Merv. The embers of resistance were stamped out in terrible fashion. For the moment a real danger had shown itself—the *jihad*, or holy war.

In whispers now the devout Mohammedans called the Mongol the " Accursed." The fire of frenzy died down. The men of Islam had a leader, but the centre of their world lay in ruins, and Jelal ed-Din, who alone could have held them together, and taken the field against the old conqueror, was chivvied round the borders by the Mongol corps of observation, and given neither time nor opportunity for assembling an army.

When the second summer came with its heat, the Khan led the greater portion of his horde up into the forested heights of the Hindu Kush, above the scorched valleys. Here he allowed them to build rest camps. The captives, nobles and slaves, judges and beggars, were set to work to raise wheat. There was no hunt this time. Sickness had taken too great a toll of the horde.

Here they could rest for a month or so in the silk pavilions of vanquished courts. The sons of Turkish *atabegs* and Persian *amirs* were their cup-bearers. The fairest women of Islam went about the camps unveiled, watched with haggard eyes by the labourers of the wheat fields, who had only the remnants of garments to cover their limbs, and must snatch their food with the dogs when the warriors ordered them to be fed.

Wild Turkomans, robbers of the caravans, came down from the heights to fraternize with the invaders and stare at the silver and gold and the endless embroidered garments that were heaped under sheds, waiting to be carried back to the Gobi. Physicians —a novelty to the nomads—were here to tend the sick, and learned men to dispute with the Cathayans while the marauders of the Gobi listened tolerantly, half understanding and little caring.

But for Genghis Khan there was the endless task of administration. Couriers came to him from the Orkhons in Cathay, and from Subotai in the Russian steppes. While he was directing military operations on these two fronts, he must keep in touch with the council of the khans in the Gobi.

Not content with messages, Genghis Khan made his Chinese councillors come to him in the Hindu

Kush, and—however they may have relished the wild ride along cliff paths and over the desert beds—no one complained.

To open up these new roads between east and west, the Khan devised the *yam* or Mongol horse-post—the pony express of thirteenth-century Asia.

CHAPTER XIX

THE ROAD MAKERS

FOR generations the Gobi clansmen had been accustomed to pass news from tent village to tent village by mounted messenger. When a man galloped up with a summons to war, or a bit of gossip, someone in the *ordu* would saddle his horse and relay the tidings to friends in the distance. These messengers were accustomed to ride fifty or sixty miles during the day.

As Genghis Khan extended his conquests, it was necessary to improve the *yam*. At first, like most of his expedients for government, it was purely a matter for the army. Permanent camps were made at intervals along the line of march, and a string of horses left at each, with youths to tend them, and a few warriors to keep off thieves. Where the horde had once passed, no stronger guard was necessary.

These camps—a few *yurts*, a shed for hay and sacks of barley in winter—were perhaps a hundred miles apart, strung along the caravan roads. Up and down this line of communication went the treasure bearers, carrying back to Karakorum the jewels, the gold ornaments, the best of the jade and enamel ware, and the great rubies of Badakshan.

Over these roads the gleanings of the horde were sent to the homeland in the Gobi. It must have been an ever-growing wonder to the nomad settlements, when each month brought its load of rarities and human beings from unknown regions. Especially when warriors who had served in Khorassan or at the edge of the inland seas rode back to sit by the *yurt* fires and relate the deeds and incredible victories of their hordes.

Nothing, perhaps, seemed incredible to the dwellers at home who had grown accustomed to having treasures brought by captured camels to their tent entrances. What did the women think of the undreamed-of luxuries, or the old men ponder as to the ride of the Orkhons out of the world as they knew it ? What became of the riches ? How did the Mongol women make use of the pearl-sewn veils of Persia ?

How greatly did the herdsmen and boys envy these returning veterans who led strings of Arab racers, and displayed from their saddlebags the silver-worked armour of a prince or *atabeg*?

The Mongols have left us no record of such experiences. But we know that they accepted the victories of the Khan as a matter predestined. Was he not the Lord *Bogdo*, the sending from the gods, the maker of laws ? Why should he not take what portion of the earth pleased him ?

Genghis Khan, apparently, did not attribute his victories to any celestial intervention. He did say, more than once, " There is only one sun in the sky, and one strength of Heaven. Only one *Kha Khan* should be upon the earth."

The veneration of his Buddhists he accepted without comment ; he acquiesced in the rôle of the Scourge of God bestowed upon him by the Moham-

medans—he even reminded them of it when he saw
something to be gained by so doing. He listened to
the urging of the astrologers, but made his own plans.
Unlike Napoleon, there was nothing of the fatalist
in him ; nor did he assume, as Alexander had done,
the attributes of a god. He set about the task of ruling
half the world with the same inflexible purpose and
patience he had devoted to tracking down a stray
horse in his youth.

He viewed titles with a utilitarian eye. Once he
ordered a letter to be written to a Mohammedan
prince on his frontier. The letter was composed by a
Persian scribe who put in all the imposing titles and
flattery beloved of the Iranians. When the missive
was read over to Genghis Khan, the old Mongol
shouted with rage and ordered it to be destroyed.

" Thou hast written foolishly," he said to the scribe.
" That prince would have thought I feared him."

And he dictated to another of his writers one of
his customary messages, brief and peremptory, and
signed " The *Kha Khan*."

To keep up communication between his armies,
Genghis Khan knit together the old caravan routes.

Officers paused at the post stations to show their
falcon tablets and to have shaggy ponies led in from
the herd. Bearded Cathayans, wrapped in voluminous
quilted coats, trotted up in two-wheeled curtained
carts, and their servants broke off bits of the precious
tea bricks to prepare over the fire. Here paused the
Ugur savants—now part and parcel of the horde—in
their high velvet hats and yellow cloaks thrown over
one shoulder.

Past the *yam* station plodded the endless lines of camels of the caravans. They carried the woven stuffs and ivory and all the goods of Islam's merchants into the desert.

The *yam* was telegraph, railroad and parcel-post all in one. It enabled newcomers from unknown regions to seek the Mongols in the Gobi. Thin-faced Jews led along the post road their laden donkeys and carts; sallow, square-chinned Armenians rode by with a curious glance at the silent Mongol soldiers sitting on their blankets by the fire, or sleeping under an opened tent flap.

These Mongols were masters of the roads. In the large towns, there would be a *daroga*, or road governor, with absolute authority in his district. With him would be a clerk, to write down the personages who called at the station, and the merchandise that went by.

The guards at the stations were so few as to be little more than an escort for the station-master. Their duties were light. Whatever they requisitioned from the countryside must be forthcoming. A Mongol had only to show himself, on his long-haired pony, with the slender lance slung over his shoulder and his lacquered armour peering from under his sable or deerskin coat—for the bystanders to hasten to him submissively. The usual petty thieves of Asia did not put in appearance. Who would dare plunder even a horse-rope from a Mongol guard post, no matter how seemingly sleepy and indifferent?

At these posts halted the weary bands of Mohammedan craftsmen, carpenters, musicians, brick makers, smiths, sword welders, or rug weavers—captives Karakorum-bound, shivering and stumbling as they crossed the wastes of the inland seas, with no more than a solitary rider of the horde as guard and guide. What chance of escape had they?

Past these posts hastened other curious bands. Yellow hat lamas, swinging their prayer wheels, their eyes fixed on remote snow summits—black hats, from the barren slopes of Tibet—the smiling, slant-eyed Buddhist pilgrims, bound to spend their years in seeking the paths once followed by their Holy One. Barefoot ascetics, long-haired *fakirs* indifferent to the world about them, and grey-garbed Nestorian priests, very full of things magical but remembering only snatches of prayer and ritual.

And often came a rider on a powerful, sweat-streaked horse, scattering priests and mandarins, and crying out one word shrilly as he reined in by the *yurts*. This man carried despatches for the Khan, and he covered a hundred and fifty miles a day without rest. For him the best horse of the station was led out swiftly.

Such was the *yam*, and two generations later Marco Polo described it as he saw it in his journey to Kambalu,* which was then the city of the Khans.

" Now you must know that the messengers of the Emperor travelling from Kambalu find at every twenty-five miles of the journey a station which they call the Horse Post House. And at each of these stations there is a large and handsome building for

---

* *Khan baligh*, the City of the King. Kubilai Khan, who was emperor in Marco Polo's time, resided in the Chinese capital. " Chandu " is Shanda—the " Xanadu " of Coleridge's poem.

    " In Xanadu did Kubla Khan
    A stately pleasure dome decree
    Where Alph the sacred river ran "—

Marco Polo relates that it took him six days' travel from Chandu to Kambalu, and his marches must have been long ones.

them to put up at. All the rooms are furnished with fine beds and rich silks. If even a king were to arrive at one of these houses, he would find himself well lodged.

"At some of these stations there shall be four hundred horses, at others two hundred. Even when the messengers have to pass through a roadless tract where no hostel stands, still the stations are to be found, although at a greater interval, and they are provided with all necessaries so that the Emperor's messengers, come from what region they may, find everything ready for them.

"Never had emperor, king, or lord such wealth as this manifests. For in all these posts there are 300,000 horses kept up, and the buildings are more than 10,000 in number. The thing is on a scale so wonderful that it is hard to bring oneself to describe it.

"In this way the emperor receives despatches from places ten days' journey off in one day and night. Many a time fruit shall be gathered at Kambalu one morning and in the evening of the next day it shall reach the Grand Khan at Chandu. The Emperor exempts these men from all tribute and pays them besides.

"Moreover there are men in these stations who, when there is a call for great haste, travel a good two hundred or two hundred and fifty miles in the day and as much in the night.* Every one of these messengers wears a great wide belt set all over with bells, so that their bells are heard jingling a long way off. And thus on reaching the post the messenger finds

* This is probably an error. The account given here is quoted, slightly condensed, from the Yule-Cordier edition of Marco Polo.

another man similarly equipped who instantly takes
over whatsoever he has in charge, and with it receives
a slip of paper from the clerk, who is always on hand
for the purpose. The clerk at each of the posts notes
the time of each courier's arrival and departure.

" They take a horse from those at the station which
are standing ready saddled, all fresh and in wind,
and mount and go at full speed. And when those at
the next post hear the bells they get ready another
horse. And the speed at which they go is marvellous.
By night, however, they can not go as fast as by day,
because they have to be accompanied by footmen with
torches.

" These couriers are highly prized ; and they could
never do it did they not bind hard the stomach, head
and chest with strong bands. And each of them carries
with him a gerfalcon tablet in sign that he is bound
on an urgent express ; so that if perchance his horse
break down, he is empowered to dismount whomso-
ever he may fall in with on the road, and take his
horse. Nobody dares refuse in such case."

The post roads were the backbone of the Khan's
administration. The Mongol *daroga* of each town
naturally had the task of keeping up the string of
horses, and levying supplies from the vicinity. Besides,
in places not actually at war with the Khan, there
was tribute to be paid to the horde. The *Yassa*, the
Code of the Khan, became the law of the land, re-
placing the Koran and the Mohammedan judges.
A census was taken.

Priests and preachers of every faith were exempt
from the tax. So ran the *Yassa*. All horses taken over

by the horde were branded with the mark of the owner, the Khan having a different brand.

To keep the census rolls, and the records of the *daroga*, the industrious Chinese or Ugurs set up the *amen* or government house. Beside the Mongol governor some dignitary of the conquered district was allowed to hold office. He served to give the Mongols information they needed, and to act as go-between.

But to a venerable sheikh in one province Genghis Khan gave a tiger tablet of authority. The sheikh could undo all the *darogas* did—could save the condemned from death. This shadow of authority extended by the Khan to the native rulers lightened the reign of terror. The time had not come yet, but would soon come, when the conquered peoples could invoke the *Yassa* as well as the Mongols. Above all things, the Mongol was consistent. After the throes of the first military occupation, he often proved a tolerant master.

But Genghis Khan spared little thought for anything except the army, the new roads, and the wealth that was flowing out of a conquered world to his people. The officers of the horde now wore the finest Turkish chain mail, and their swords were of Damascus forging. Except for his constant curiosity as to new weapons and new knowledge, the Khan heeded little the luxury of Islam. He kept the dress and the habits of the Gobi.

He could be indulgent at times. But he was moody and intent on finishing the half-completed work of conquest. His terrible flashes of temper were frequent. He made quite a favourite of a peculiarly

M

hideous-looking physician of Samarkand, who treated his eyes for him. The man, waxing bold in the Khan's tolerance, began to be something of a nuisance to the Mongol officers. He asked for a particular singing girl of beauty who had been captured in the storming of Urgench.

The Khan, amused by his insistence, ordered the girl to be given to him. The ugliness of the physician proved distasteful to the beautiful captive, and the man of Samarkand came to the Khan again, to plead that she should be made to obey him. This angered the old Mongol, who launched into a tirade on men who could not enforce obedience, and who turned traitor. Then he had the physician put to death.

In this autumn Genghis Khan had summoned the higher officers to the usual council, but Juchi, his eldest son, had not come—had sent instead a gift of horses with the explanation that he was sick.

Some of the princes of the horde disliked Juchi, held up to him the stigma of his birth, called him " Tatar." And they pointed out to the Khan that his eldest son had disobeyed the summons to the *kurultai*. The old Mongol sent for the officer who had brought the horses and asked whether Juchi were really sick.

" I do not know," the man from Kipchak answered, " but he was hunting when I left him."

Angered, the Khan retired to his tent, and his officers expected that he would march against Juchi, who had committed the crime of disobedience. Instead, he dictated a message to one of his writers, and gave it to a courier who started west. He was not willing to divide the horde, and very probably he hoped that his son would not rebel against him, because he had ordered Subotai to return from Europe,* and to bring Juchi to his headquarters, wherever he might be.

* See Note X, Correspondence between the European Monarchs and the Mongols. page 239.

CHAPTER XX

THERE was little time for anything except action
that eventful autumn. Herat and the other
cities rose against the conquerors. Jelal ed-Din was
mustering an army in the east—so messages from the
corps of observation along the Hindu Kush reported.
Genghis Khan was planning to send Tuli, his most
dependable leader, after the Kharesmian prince, when
he heard of the rising in Herat. Instead, he sent Tuli
west into Khorassan with several divisions.

Genghis Khan took the field with 60,000 men to
find and destroy the new Kharesmian army. He found
in his path the strong city of Bamiyan in the Koh-i-
Baba ranges. He settled down to invest it, sending the
greater part of his forces under another Orkhon to
meet Jelal ed-Din.

In due course couriers arrived at Bamiyan with
word that Jelal ed-Din had 60,000 men with him—
that the Mongol general had come in contact with
him, and had avoided several attempts of the Kharesmians to ambush him. Scouts were watching the
movements of the redoubtable prince.

What had happened was that an Afghan army had
joined Jelal ed-Din in this crisis, doubling his strength.
Word came in not long after that the Turks and

Afghans had defeated the Mongol Orkhon, driving his men into the mountains.

Genghis Khan turned with new fury to the city before him. The defenders had laid bare all the district, even removing the large stones that could be used in siege engines. The Mongols had not the usual equipment with them, and their wooden towers, raised against the walls, were fired by arrows and flaming naphtha—until the cattle were slaughtered and their hides used to cover the wood frames.

The Khan ordered an assault—the storm that is not to be abandoned until the city is taken. At this point one of his grandsons, who had followed him under the walls, was killed. The old Mongol ordered the body of the child—whom he had liked for his courage—to be carried back to the tents.

He urged on the assault, and, throwing off his helmet, pushed through his ranks until he was at the head of a storming party. They gained footing in a breach, and Bamiyan fell to them not long after. Every living being was slain within its walls, and mosques and palaces pulled down. Even the Mongols spoke of Bamiyan as *Mou-baligh*, the City of Sorrow.

But Genghis Khan left it at once to assemble his scattered divisions. They were feeling their way toward him through the hills, not much the worse for their drubbing. The Khan rallied them, and praised their devotion. Instead of blaming the unhappy Orkhon who had been worsted by Jelal ed-Din, he rode back with him over the scene of the action, asking what had happened and pointing out the mistakes he had made.

The Kharesmian prince did not prove himself as

able in victory as he had been sturdy in defeat. He had his moment of exultation when his men tortured to death the Mongol prisoners and divided up the captured horses and weapons ; but the Afghans quarrelled with his officers and left him.

Genghis Khan was on the march against him, after detaching an army to watch the movements of the Afghans. Jelal ed-Din retreated east to Ghazna, but the Mongols were hard after him. He sent messengers to summon new allies, but these found that the Mongols had guarded the mountain passes. With his thirty thousand men Jelal ed-Din hurried down through the foothills and out upon the valley of the Indus.

His hope was to cross the river and league himself with the sultans of Delhi. But the Mongols, who had been five days behind him at Ghazna, were now within half a day's ride. Genghis Khan had barely allowed his men to dismount to cook their food.

Desperate now, the Kharesmian prince hastened to the river, found that he had come to a place where the Indus was too swift and deep for the crossing, and turned at bay, his left flank protected by a mountain ridge, his right by a bend of the river.

The chivalry of Islam, hunted out of its own lands, prepared to measure its strength against the inexorable Mongol. Jelal ed-Din ordered all the boats along the bank to be destroyed, so his men would not think of fleeing. His position was strong, but he must hold it or be annihilated.

At dawn the Mongols advanced all along the line. They had emerged out of the darkness in formation, Genghis Khan with his standard, and the ten thousand cavalry of the imperial guard in reserve behind the centre. These, at first, were not engaged.

The impetuous Kharesmian prince was the first to send his men forward. His right wing—always the strongest division in a Mohammedan army of that day—under Emir Malik skirmished with the left of the Khan, and drove home a charge along the bank of the Indus that forced the Mongols back at this point. They scattered into squadrons as usual, re-formed under one of the Khan's sons, and were forced back again.

On their right, the Mongols had been checked by the barrier of the lofty and barren ridges, and here they halted. Jelal ed-Din detached forces from this part of his line to aid the advancing right wing of Emir Malik. And later in the day he withdrew still more squadrons from the defenders of the mountain to strengthen his centre.

Determined to risk everything in one cast of fortune, he charged with the *élite* of his host, straight into the Mongol centre, cutting through to the standard, seeking the Khan. The old Mongol was not there. His horse had been killed under him and he had mounted another and gone elsewhere.

It was a moment of apparent victory for the Kharesmian, and the ululation of the Mohammedans rose above the din of beating hoofs, the grinding of steel, and the cries of the wounded.

The Mongol centre, badly shaken by the charge, kept on fighting stubbornly. Genghis Khan had noticed the withdrawal of nearly all the Kharesmian left wing, posted on the heights. He ordered a *tuman* commander, Bela Noyon, to go with the guides he had been questioning and to cross the mountain at all costs. It was the old turning movement of the Mongols, the standard-sweep.

The *noyon* with his men followed the guides into sheer gorges and ascended cliff paths that seemed impassable. Some of the warriors fell into the chasms, but the greater part gained the ridge late in the day and descended on the remnant of men left by Jelal ed-Din to protect this point. Over the mountain barrier the Kharesmian flank was turned. Bela Noyon charged into the enemy camp.

Meanwhile Genghis Khan had taken the leadership of his ten thousand heavy cavalry, and had gone— not to the menaced centre, but to the defeated left wing. His charge against Emir Malik's forces routed them. Wasting no time in following them up, the Khan swung his squadrons about and drove them against the flank of Jelal ed-Din's troops of the centre. He had cut off the wing by the river from the Kharesmian prince.

The stout hearted but wearying Mohammedans had been rendered helpless by the sagacity of the old Mongol, and by manœuvring as perfect as the final moves of a checkmate. And the end came swiftly, inexorably. ✻ Jelal ed-Din made a last and hopeless charge against the horsemen of the guard, and tried to withdraw his men toward the river. He was followed up, his squadrons broken ; Bela Noyon pressed in upon him, and when he gained the steep bank of the Indus at last, he had around him no more than seven hundred followers.

Realizing that the end had come, he mounted a fresh horse, rid himself of his armour, and with only his sword and bow and a quiver of arrows, he forced his charger over the edge of the bank, plunging into the swift current, and making for the distant shore.

Genghis Khan had given orders that the prince was to be taken alive. The Mongols had drawn in upon the last Kharesmians and the Khan lashed his horse through the fighting to watch the rider he had seen leap from the twenty-foot bank. For a while he gazed in silence at Jelal ed-Din. Putting his finger to his lips he uttered an ungrudged exclamation of praise.

"Fortunate should be the father of such a son!"

Though he could admire the daring of the Kharesmian prince, he did not intend to spare Jelal ed-Din. Some of his Mongols wished to try to swim after their foe, but the Khan would not allow this. He watched Jelal ed-Din reach the far bank, in spite of current and waves. The next day he sent a *tuman* in pursuit where the river could be crossed, giving this task to Bela Noyon, the same officer who had led a division over the cliff paths to the Kharesmian camp.

Bela Noyon ravaged Multan and Lahore, picked up the trail of the fugitive, but lost him among the multitudes upon the way to Delhi. The oppressive heat astonished the men from the Gobi plateau and the *noyon* turned back at length, saying to the Khan:

"The heat of this place slays men, and the water is neither fresh nor clear."

So India—all except this northern segment—was spared the Mongol conquest. Jelal ed-Din survived, but his moment had passed. He fought against the horde again, but as a partisan, an adventurer without a country.

The battle of the Indus was the last stand of the Kharesmian chivalry. From Tibet to the Caspian sea resistance had ceased, and the survivors of the peoples of Islam had become the slaves of the conqueror. And with the end of warfare, as in Cathay, the thoughts of the old Mongol turned to his homeland.

" My sons will live to desire such lands and cities as these," he said, " but I cannot."

He was needed in far Asia. Muhuli had died after binding more firmly the Mongol yoke upon the Chinese ; in the Gobi the council of the khans was restless and bickering ; in the kingdoms of Hia rebellion smouldered. Genghis Khan led his horde up the Indus. He knew that Hia, on the far slopes of Tibet, could be no more than eight hundred miles distant, when he entered the long valleys of Kashmir. But, as Alexander had done before him, he found the road blocked by the *massifs* of impenetrable ranges. Wiser than Alexander in his disappointment, he turned back without hesitation and set out to retrace his steps around the Roof of the World, to the caravan route that he had opened in his invasion.

He stormed Peshawar and route-marched back to Samarkand. In the spring of 1220 he had first seen the walls and gardens of Samarkand, and now, in the autumn of 1221, his task under the Roof of the World had ended.

" It is time," the sage, Ye Liu Chutsai, agreed, " to make an end of slaying."

When the horde left the last ruins of the south behind them the Khan gave the accustomed order to put to death all captives, and in this way perished the unhappy multitude that had followed the nomads.

The women of Mohammedan monarchs, who were to be taken to the Gobi, were placed at the roadside to wail the last sight of their native land.

For a moment, it seems, the old Mongol pondered the meaning of his conquests.

"Dost thou think," he asked a savant of Islam, "that the blood I have shed will be remembered against me by mankind?" He recalled the higher wisdom of Cathay and Islam that he had tried to understand, and had dismissed incuriously. "I have pondered the wisdom of the sages. I see now I have slain without knowledge of what to do rightly. But what care I for such men?"

To the refugees gathered in Samarkand, who came out to meet him in fear, bringing gifts, he was kind. He talked with them, explained anew the short-comings of their late Shah, who had neither known how to keep his promise nor defend his people. He appointed governors from among them and extended to them what might be called suffrage in the Mongol dominion—a share in the protection of the *Yassa*. These people would be ruled, before very long, by his sons.

The conqueror was feeling the bite of old wounds, and seemed to understand that his time in the world was approaching its end. He wished to have things in order—rebellion quenched, the *Yassa* enforced, and his sons in authority.

He sent out over the post roads a summons to all high officers to attend a great council on the river Syr, near the spot where he had first entered Kharesm.

CHAPTER XXI

THE COURT OF THE PALADINS

THE place chosen for the gathering was a meadow seven leagues in circuit—a place ideal to a Mongol's thinking because water fowl filled the marshes by the river ; golden pheasants flitted through the lush grass. Abundant grazing—game to be hunted over the downs. The time was early spring, the customary month of the *kurultai.*

And, punctual to the summons, the leaders of the hordes began to arrive. Only the industrious Subotai, recalled from Europe, was a little late.

They came in from all the quarters of the four winds, Eagles of the empire, generals from far frontiers, roving *tar-khans*, subject kings and ambassadors. They had journeyed far to this Camelot of the nomad peers. And they brought with them no mean retinue. The *kibitkas* from Cathay were drawn by matched yokes of oxen and covered with silk. On their platforms fluttered captured banners.

The officers from the slopes of Tibet had their covered wagons gilded and lacquered, drawn by lines of ponderous, long-haired yaks with wide horns and silky white tails—animals greatly prized by the Mongols. Tuli, Master of War, coming up from Khorassan, brought with him strings of white camels. Chatagai, descending from the snows of the ranges

A PERSIAN HUNTING SCENE EARLY SEVENTEENTH CENTURY
This shows the types of weapons used for the chase

drove in a hundred thousand horses. They were clad, these officers of the hordes, in cloth-of-gold and silver, covered with sable coats, and wraps of silver-grey wolfskins to protect their finery.

From the T'ian shan came the Idikut of the Ugurs, the most cherished of all allies, and the Lion King of the Christian folk—broad-faced Kirghiz chieftains coming to render their allegiance to the conqueror—long-limbed Turkomans in stately robes.

The horses, instead of weather-stained leather, were barded in jingling chain mail, their harness bright with polished silver work and afire with jewels.

From the Gobi appeared a much-prized youngster, Kubilai, the son of Tuli, now nine years old. He had been allowed to join in his first hunt, an important event for this grandson of an emperor. Genghis Khan with his own hand completed the ceremony of initiation.

The leaders of the hordes now gathered in the *kurultai* place, a white pavilion so large that it sheltered two thousand men. It had one entrance to be used by no one except the Khan ; the warriors bearing shields at the great entrance facing south were merely a routine guard mount. So rigid was discipline in the hordes, and so firmly established was the routine of the empire, that no unauthorized person ventured within the quarters of the conqueror.

As they had once brought to the Khan captured horses and women and weapons in the Gobi, the chiefs of the hordes and the subject kings now offered him their gifts of a new sort, the best of the treasure gleaned carefully from half the earth. " Never," says the chronicler, " was such splendour seen before."

Instead of mare's milk, the princes of the empire
had mead of honey and the red and white wines of
Persia. The Khan himself admitted a fondness for
the wines of Shiraz.

He sat now in the gold throne of Mohammed that
he had brought with him from Samarkand ; beside it
rested the sceptre and crown of the dead emperor of
Islam. When the council gathered, the mother of the
Shah was led in, chains on her wrists. But under the
throne was placed a square of grey felt woven out of
animal hair, as a symbol of his old authority in the
Gobi.

To the assembled leaders out of the east, he
recounted the campaigns of the last three years. " I
have gained great mastery," he said gravely, " by
virtue of the *Yassa*. Live ye in obedience to the
laws."

The shrewd Mongol wasted no words in boasting
of his achievements ; the thing to be gained was
obedience to the law. He no longer needed to advise
and lead his officers in person. They were able to
wage war on their own account, and he saw clearly
the grave danger of a division among them. To
emphasize the extent of his conquests, he had all the
visiting ambassadors ushered to the throne one by one.

To his three sons he spoke a word of warning.
" Do not allow quarrels to come between you. Be
faithful and unfailing to Ogotai."

After that there was feasting for a month in the
kurultai, and to this concourse came two most welcome
guests. Subotai rode in from the borderland of
Poland, bringing with him Juchi.

Juchi, the first-born, had been sought out by the

veteran Orkhon who persuaded him to attend the council and to face his father again. So Juchi appeared before the Khan and knelt to press his hand to his forehead. The old conqueror, who was deeply attached to Juchi, was gratified—though he made no display of affection. The conqueror of the steppes had brought as a gift to his sire a hundred thousand Kipchak horses. Disliking the court, Juchi asked for permission to return to the Volga, and this was granted him.

The concourse broke up, Chatagai riding back to his mountains, and the other hordes taking the trail to Karakorum. The chronicler relates that every day of the journey, Genghis Khan summoned Subotai to come to his side and relate his adventures in the western world.

CHAPTER XXII

THE END OF THE TASK

GENGHIS KHAN was not destined to spend his last years in his homeland. All had been prepared for his sons but two things. Two hostile powers still survived in the world as the old Khan knew it—the troublesome king of Hia near Tibet and the ancient Sung in southern China. He passed a season at Karakorum among his people with Bourtai at his side, and then he was in the saddle again. Subotai was sent to invade the lands of the Sung, and Genghis Khan took upon himself the task of quelling the desert clans of Hia for ever.

This he did. Marching in winter through frozen swamps, he found his foes of other days drawn up to receive him—remnants of Cathayans, armies of western China, Turks and all the forces of Hia. The chronicle gives us a glimpse of the grim pageant of destruction—fur-clad Mongols fighting across the ice of a river, the allies, seemingly victorious, charging *en masse* upon the veterans of the Khan's centre, the heart of the horde. Three hundred thousand men may have perished here.

And then the aftermath. Tricked, shaken, and hunted down, the remaining warriors of the allies fleeing. All men capable of bearing arms put to death in the path of the horde. The king of Hia, escaped to a mountain citadel, guarded by snow-drifted gorges, sending his submission to the inexorable Khan, hiding his hatred and despair under the mask of friendship, asking that the past be forgotten.

"Say to your master," Genghis Khan replied to the envoys, "that I have no wish to remember what is past. I will hold him in friendship."

But the Khan would not make an end of war. There were the people of the Sung to be humbled, as the allies had been. The horde marched in mid-winter toward the boundaries of ancient China. Ye Liu Chutsai, the sage, dared to protest against the annihilation of the Sung.

"If these people be slain, how then will they aid thee, or make wealth for thy sons?"

The old conqueror pondered, remembering perhaps that after he had made deserts of once populous lands the sages of Cathay had helped to keep things in order. He answered unexpectedly, "Be thou, then, master of subject peoples—serve thou my sons faithfully."

He would not forgo the military conquest of the Sung. That must be finished, to the end. He kept his saddle and led his armies across the Yellow river. Here the Khan learned of the death of Juchi in the steppes. He said that he wished to be alone in his tent, and he grieved heavily in silence for his first-born.

Not long since, when Ogotai's little son had been slain beside him at Bamiyan, the Khan had commanded the bereaved father not to show sorrow. "Obey me in this thing. Thy son is slain. I forbid thee to weep!"

N

Nor did he himself show outwardly that the death of Juchi troubled him. The hordes went forward, the routine was as usual, but the Khan spoke less with his officers and it was noticed that the tidings of a fresh victory near the Caspian failed to rouse him, or to draw either comment or praise from him. When the horde entered a dense fir forest where snow lay still in the shadows, although the sun was warm, he gave command to halt.

He ordered couriers to ride swiftly to his nearest son, Tuli, who was camped not far away. When the Master of War, now a man grown, dismounted at the *yurt* of the Khan, he found his father lying upon a carpet near the fire, wrapped in felt and sable robes.

" It is clear to me," the old Mongol greeted the prince, " that I must leave everything and go hence from thee."

He had been sick for some time, and this sickness, he knew now, was draining away his life. He ordered to his side the general officers of the horde, and while they knelt with Tuli, listening intently to his words, he gave them clear directions how to carry on the war against the Sung that he had begun but could not finish. Tuli, especially, was to take over all lands in the east, as Chatagai was to do in the west, while Ogotai must be supreme over them, the Kha Khan at Karakorum.

Like the nomad he was, he died uncomplaining, leaving to his sons the greatest of empires and the most destructive of armies, as if his possessions had been no more than tents and herds. This was in the year 1227, the Year of the Mouse in the Cycle of the Twelve Beasts.

The chronicle tells us that Genghis Khan made provision in his last illness for the destruction of the Hia king, his old foeman, who was then on his way to the horde. The Khan commanded that his death be kept secret until this could be done.

A spear was thrust, point in the earth, before the white *yurt* of the conqueror which stood apart from the rest of the camp. The astrologers and sages who came to wait upon the Khan were kept without by guards, and only the high officers came and went through the entrance, as if their leader were indisposed and giving orders from his bed. When the Hia monarch and his train reached the Mongols, the visitors were invited to a feast, given robes of honour and seated among the officers of the horde. Then they were slain, to a man.

Deprived of Genghis Khan, awe-struck at the death of the seemingly invincible man who had made them masters of all they could desire, the Orkhons and princes of the horde turned back to escort the body to the Gobi. Before burial it must be shown to his people and carried to the abiding place of Bourtai, the first wife.

Genghis Khan had died in the lands of the Sung, and to prevent his foemen from discovering the loss of the Mongols, the warriors escorting the death car cut down all the people they met until they reached the edge of the desert. There the men of the horde, the veterans of long warfare, mourned aloud as they rode beside the funeral car.

To them it seemed incredible that the great Khan should have ceased to go before the standard, and

that they were no longer to be sent hither and thither
at his will.

"O Lord *bogdo*," cried a grey-haired *tar-khan*,
"wilt thou leave us thus? Thy birth-land and its
rivers await thee, thy fortunate land with thy golden
house surrounded by thy heroes await thee. Why hast
thou left us in this warm land, where so many foemen
lie dead?"

Others took up the mourning as they crossed the
bed of the barrens. In this way the chronicler has
written down their lament:

> "*Aforetime thou didst swoop like a falcon; now a rumbling
> cart bears thee onward,*
> > *O my Khan!*
>
> "*Hast thou in truth left thy wife and children, and the
> council of thy people?*
> > *O my Khan!*
>
> "*Wheeling in pride like an eagle, once thou didst lead us;
> but now thou hast stumbled and fallen,*
> > *O my Khan!*"

The conqueror was brought home, not to Karakorum, but to the valleys where he had struggled for
life as a boy, to the heritage that he would not desert.
The couriers of the hordes mounted and galloped off
into the prairies, bearing word to the Orkhons and
princes and the distant generals that Genghis Khan
was dead.

When the last officer had come in and dismounted
at the death *yurt*, the body was taken to its resting
place—most probably to the forest he himself had
selected. No one knows the exact burial place. The
grave was dug under a great tree.

The Mongols say that a certain clan was exempted from military duty and charged to watch the site*, and that incense was burned unceasingly in the grove until the surrounding forest grew so thick that the tall tree was lost among its fellows and all trace of the grave*† vanished.

* A descendant of the conqueror, the Prince of Kalachin, believes that the great Khan was buried in the Ordou country, between the loop of the Hoang and the Wall, near Etjen Koro, and that every year the Mongols hold ceremonies at the grave, bringing hither the sword and the saddle and the bow of Genghis Khan. There is also a legend among the Mongols that every year a white horse appears at the grave

*† See Note XI, The Tomb of Genghis Khan, page 243.

Part IV

AFTERWORD

TWO years passed in mourning. During these two years Tuli remained in Karakorum as regent, and at the end of the appointed time the princes and generals journeyed back into the Gobi, to select the new Kha Khan, or emperor, in obedience to the wishes of the dead conqueror.

They came as monarchs in their own right—the right of heritage, by the will of Genghis Khan. Chatagai, the harsh tempered—now the eldest son—from Central Asia and all the Mohammedan lands : Ogotai, the good humoured, from the Gogi plains : Batu, the " Splendid," the son of Juchi, from the steppes of Russia.

They had grown from youth to manhood as Mongol clansmen ; now they were masters of portions of the world, with its riches, that they had not known existed. They were Asiatics, raised among barbarians ; every one of the four had a powerful army at his summons. They had tasted the wine of luxury in their new dominions. " My descendants," Genghis Khan had said, " will clothe themselves in embroidered gold stuffs ; they will nourish themselves with meats, and will mount splendid horses. They will press in their arms young and fair women, and they will not

think of that to which they owe all these desirable
things."

Nothing was more natural than that they should
have quarrelled and gone to war over their heritage.
It was almost inevitable, after those two years—
especially in the case of Chatagai, who was now the
eldest, and entitled by Mongol custom to claim the
khanship. But the will of the dead conqueror had
been impressed upon all this multitude. The discipline
established by an iron hand still held them bound
together. Obedience—fidelity to their brothers—and
the end of quarrelling—the *Yassa* itelf !

Many times Genghis Khan had warned them that
their dominion would vanish and they themselves be
lost if they did not agree. He had understood that
this new empire could be held together only by
submission to the authority of one man. And he
had chosen not the warlike Tuli, or the inflexible
Chatagai, but the generous and guileless Ogotai as
his successor. Keen understanding of his sons had
dictated this choice. Chatagai would never have
submitted to Tuli, the youngest ; and the Master of
War would not long have served his harsh elder
brother.

When the princes assembled at Karakorum, Tuli,
the *Ulugh Noyon*, Greatest of Nobles, resigned his
regency, and Ogotai was asked to accept the throne.
The Master of Counsel refused, saying it was not
fitting for him to be honoured above his uncles and
elder brother. Either because Ogotai was obstinate or
because the soothsayers were unfavourable, forty days
passed in uncertainty and anxiety. Then the Orkhons
and elder warriors waited upon Ogotai and spoke to

him angrily. " What doest thou ? The Khan himself hath chosen thee for his successor ! "

Tuli added his voice—repeated the last words of his father, and Ye Liu Chutsai, the sage Cathayan, master of the treasury, used all his wit in averting a possible calamity. Tuli, troubled, asked the astrologer-minister if this day were not unfavourable.

" After this," responded the Cathayan at once, " no day will be favourable."

He urged Ogotai to mount without delay to the gold throne on the felt-covered dais, and as the new emperor was doing so, Ye Liu Chutsai went to his side and spoke to Chatagai.

" Thou art the elder," he said, " but thou art a subject. Being the elder, seize this moment to be the first to prostrate thyself before the Throne."

An instant's hesitation and Chatagai threw himself down before his brother. All the officers and nobles in the council pavilion followed his example, and Ogotai was acknowledged Kha Khan. The throng went out and bent their heads to the south, toward the sun, and the multitude of the camp did likewise. Then followed days of feasting. The treasure that Genghis Khan had left, the riches gathered from all the corners of unknown lands, were given to the other princes, the officers and Mongols of the army.* Ogotai pardoned all men accused of wrong-doing since the death of his father. He reigned tolerantly for a Mongol of that day, and heeded the advice of Ye Liu Chutsai,*† who laboured with heroic fortitude

---

* A legend exists that forty fair young women in jewelled garments and forty fine stallions were taken to the grave of Genghis Khan and there slain.
*† See Notes XII and XIII, Ye Liu Chutsai and Ogotai, pages 245 and 248.

to consolidate the empire of his masters on the one hand, and to restrain, on the other hand, the Mongols from further annihilation of human beings. He dared oppose the terrible Subotai at a time when the Orkhon—who was carrying on war in the lands of the Sung with Tuli—wished to massacre the inhabitants of a great city. "During all these years in Cathay," the wise chancellor argued, "our armies have lived upon the crops and the riches of these people. If we destroy the men, what will the bare land avail us?"

Ogotai conceded the point and the lives of a million and a half Chinese who had flocked into the city were spared. It was Ye Liu Chutsai who put the tribute gathering in regular form—one head of cattle for every hundred from the Mongols, and a certain sum in silver or silk from every family of Cathay. He argued Ogotai into appointing lettered Cathayans to high office in the treasury and administration.

"To make a vase," he suggested, "thou dost avail thyself of a potter. To keep accounts and records, learned men should be used."

"Well," retorted the Mongol, "what hinders thee from making use of them?"

While Ogotai built himself a new palace, Ye Liu Chutsai established schools for young Mongols. Five hundred wagons drove in each day to Karakorum, now known as *Ordu-baligh*, the Court City. These carts brought provisions, grain and precious goods to the storehouses and treasury of the emperor. The rule of the desert khans was firmly fastened upon half the world.

Unlike the empire of Alexander, the dominion of the Mongol conqueror remained intact after his death. He had made the Mongol clans obedient to one ruler ; he had given them a rigid code of laws, primitive, but well adapted to his purpose, and during his military overlordship he had laid the foundations for the administration of the empire. In this last task, Ye Liu Chutsai was of priceless aid.

Perhaps the greatest heritage the conqueror left his sons was the Mongol army. By his will, Ogotai, Chatagai and Tuli divided up his main horde—his personal army, as it might be called. But the system of mobilization, of training, and manœuvring in war remained as Genghis Khan had formed it. Moreover, in Subotai and others, the sons of the conqueror had veteran generals quite equal to the task of extending the empire.

He had instilled into his sons and his subjects the idea that the Mongols were the natural masters of the world, and he had so broken the resistance of the strongest empires that the completion of the work was a comparatively simple matter for them—and Subotai. It might be called mopping up after the first advance.

In the early years of Ogotai's reign a Mongol general, Charmagan, defeated Jelal ed-Din and put an end to him for ever—and consolidated the regions west of the Caspian, such as Armenia. At the same time Subotai and Tuli advanced far south of the Hoang Ho and subdued the remnants of the Chins.

In 1235 Ogotai held a council, and it resulted in the

second great wave of Mongol conquest. Batu, first Khan of the Golden Horde, was sent with Subotai into the west, to the sorrow of Europe as far as the Adriatic and the gates of Vienna.* Other armies took the field in Korea, China and southern Persia. This wave withdrew upon the death of Ogotai in 1241—Subotai being again wrenched back by the inflexible summons from his goal, Europe.

The ten years that followed were full of cross-currents, the growing feud between the house of Chatagai and that of Ogotai—the brief appearance of Kuyuk, who may or may not have been a Nestorian Christian, but who ruled through Christian ministers, one of them the son of Ye Liu Chutsai, and who had a chapel built before his tent. Then the rule passed from the house of Ogotai to the sons of Tuli—Mangu and Kubilai Khan.*† And the third and most exten-sive wave of conquest swept the world.

Hulagu, the brother of Kubilai, aided by Subotai's son, invaded Mesopotamia, took Baghdad and Damas-cus—breaking for ever the power of the Kalifates—and came almost within sight of Jerusalem. Antioch, held by the descendants of Christian crusaders, became subject to the Mongols, who entered Asia Minor as far as Smyrna, and within a week's march of Con-stantinople.

At almost the same time Kubilai launched his armada against Japan, and extended his frontiers down to the Malay states, and beyond Tibet into Bengal. His reign (1259 to 1294) was the golden age of the

---

* " *La paix qui regnait dans le fond de l'Orient devint funeste à l' Europe* "
—Abel Rémusat. See note on Subotai in Europe.
*† Note XIV, The Last Court of the Nomads, page 252.

Mongols.* Kubilai departed from the customs of his fathers, moved the court to Cathay, and made himself more a Chinese in habits than a Mongol.*† He ruled with moderation and treated his subject peoples with humanity. Marco Polo has left us a vivid picture of his court.

But the change of the court to Cathay was an omen of the break-up of the central empire. The Il-khans of Persia—Hulagu's descendants, who reached their greatest power under Ghazan Khan about 1300— were at too great a distance from the Kha Khan to be in touch with him. Besides, they were fast becoming Mohammedans. Such, also, was the situation of the Golden Horde near Russia. Kubilai's Mongols were being converted to Buddhism. Religious and political wars followed the death of this grandson of Genghis Khan. The Mongol empire dissolved gradually into separate kingdoms.

About 1400 a Turkish conqueror, Timur-i-lang (Tamerlane) brought together the central Asian and Persian fragments, and trounced the Golden Horde founded by Batu the son of Juchi.

Until 1368 the Mongols remained masters of China, and it was 1555 before they lost their last strongholds in Russia to Ivan Grodznoi (the Terrible). Around the Caspian sea their descendants, the Uzbegs, were a power under Shaibani in 1500, and drove Babar the Tiger, a descendant of Genghis Khan, into India, where he made himself the first of the great Moghuls.

---

* " He ruled over a wider extent than any Mongol or indeed any other sovereign. He was the first to govern by peaceful means. The splendour of his court and the magnificence of his entourage easily surpassed that of any Western ruler."—*The Cambridge Medieval History*, Vol. IV, p. 645.

*† See Note XV, The Grandson of Genghis Khan in the Holy Land, page 265.

GHAZAN THE II KHAN OF PERSIA SEVERAL GENERATIONS AFTER GENGHIS KHAN

It was the middle of the eighteenth century, six hundred years after the birth of Genghis Khan, before the last scions of the conqueror relinquished their strongholds.   Then, in Hindustan, the Moghuls * gave way to the British, the Mongols in the east yielded to the armies of the illustrious Chinese emperor, K'ien lung.

The Tatar khans of the Crimea became the subjects of Catherine the Great at the same time that the unfortunate Kalmuk or Torgut horde evacuated its pastures on the Volga and started the long and dreadful march eastward to its former home—a march vividly pictured by De Quincey in his *Flight of a Tatar Tribe*.

A glance at a map of Asia in the mid-eighteenth century will show the final refuge of the nomad clansmen, descendants of the horde of Genghis Khan. In the vast spaces between stormy Lake Baïkul and the salt sea of Aral—barely charted in the maps of that day, and marked vaguely "Tartary" or "Independent Tartary"—in the ranges of the mid-continent, they wandered from summer to winter pasture, living in their felt *yurts*, driving their herds—Karaïts, Kalmuks and Mongols, utterly unaware that through these same valleys Prester John of Asia had once fled to his death, and the yak-tail standard of Genghis Khan had advanced to terrify the world.

In this fashion ended the Mongol empire, dissolving into the nomad clans from which it had sprung, leaving remnants of peaceful herdsmen where warriors had once massed.

* Moghuls—so the first Europeans to visit India pronounced the word Mongol.

The brief and terrible pageant of the Mongol horsemen has passed almost without trace. The desert city of Karakorum is buried under the sand-waves of the barrens ; the grave of Genghis Khan lies hidden somewhere in a forest near one of the rivers of his birthplace ; the riches he gathered from his conquest were given to the men that served him. No tomb marks the burial place of Bourtai, the wife of his youth. No Mongol *literati* of his day gathered the events of his life into an epic.

His achievement is recorded for the most part by his enemies. So devastating was his impact upon civilization that virtually a new beginning had to be made in half the world. The empire of Cathay, of Prester John, of Black Cathay, of Kharesm, and—after his death—the Kalifate of Baghdad, of Russia, and for a while the principalities of Poland, ceased to be. When this indomitable barbarian conquered a nation all other warfare came to an end. The whole scheme of things, whether sorry or otherwise, was altered, and among the survivors of a Mongol conquest peace endured for a long time.

The blood-feuds of the grand princes of ancient Russia—lords of Twer and Vladimir and Susdal, were buried under a greater calamity. All these figures of an elder world appear to us only as shadows. Empires crumbled under the Mongol avalanche, and monarchs fled to their death in wild fear. What would have happened if Genghis Khan had not lived, we do not know.

What did happen was that the Mongol, like the Roman peace, enabled culture to spring up anew. Nations had been shuffled to and fro—or rather the remnants of them—Mohammedan science and skill carried bodily into the Far East, Chinese inventiveness and administrative ability had penetrated into the west. In the devastated gardens of Islam, scholars and architects enjoyed, if not a golden, a silver age under the Mongol Il-khans; and the thirteenth century was notable in China for its literature, especially plays, and its magnificence—the century of the Yuan.

When political coherence began again after the retreat of the Mongol hordes, something very natural but quite unexpected happened. Out of the ruins of the warring Russian princedoms emerged the empire of Ivan the Great, and China, united for the first time by the Mongols, appeared as a single dominion.

With the coming of the Mongols and their foes the Mamluks, the long chapter of the crusades ended. For a while under Mongol overlordship, Christian pilgrims could visit the Holy Sepulchre in safety, and Mohammedans the temple of Solomon. For the first time the priests of Europe could venture into far Asia, and venture they did, looking about them in vain for the old Man of the Mountain who had harried the crusaders, and the kingdoms of Prester John and Cathay.

In this vast shaking up of human beings, perhaps the most vital result was the destruction of the growing power of Islam. With the host of Kharesm disappeared the main military strength of the Mohammedans, and with Baghdad and Bokhara the old culture of the Kalifs and *imams*. Arabic ceased to be the universal language of scholars in half the world. The Turks were driven west, and one clan, the Othmans (Ottomans, so called) became in time the masters of Constantinople. A red hat lama, called out of Tibet to preside at the coronation of Kubilai, brought with him out of his mountains the hierarchy of the priests of Lhassa.

Genghis Khan, the destroyer, had broken down the barriers of the Dark Ages. He had opened up roads. Europe came into contact with the arts of Cathay. At the court of his son, Armenian princes and Persian grandees rubbed shoulders with Russian princes.

A general reshuffling of ideas followed the opening of the roads. An abiding curiosity about far Asia stirred Europeans. Marco Polo followed Fra Rubruquis to Kambalu. Two centuries later Vasco da Gama set forth to find his way by sea to the Indies. Columbus sailed to reach, not America, but the land of the Great Khan.

Notes

I

THE grim pageantry of death that appeared in the tracks of the Mongol horsemen has not been painted in continuous detail in this volume. The slaughter that cast whole peoples into death-throes is well depicted in the general histories of the Mongols, written by Europeans, Mohammedans and Chinese. Little allusion is made here to such scenes of carnage as the blotting out of Kiev, the Court of the Golden Heads, as the Mongols called the ancient Byzantine citadel with its gilt domes. Here the torturing of old people, the ravishing of younger women, and the hunting down of children ended in utter desolation that was rendered more ghastly by the following pestilence and famine. The effluvium of festering bodies was so great that even the Mongols avoided such places and named them *Mou-baligh*, City of Woe.

The student of history will find vital significance in this unprecedented maiming and subsequent rebuilding of human races. The impact of the Mongols, brought about by Genghis Khan, has been well summed up by the authors of the *Cambridge Medieval History*.

" Unchecked by human valour, they were able to overcome the terrors of vast deserts, the barriers of mountains and seas, the severities of climate, and the ravages of famine and pestilence. No dangers could appal them, no stronghold could resist them, no prayer for mercy could move them. . . . We are confronted with a new power in history, with a force that was to bring to an abrupt end as a *deus ex machina*, many dramas that would otherwise have ended in a deadlock, or would have dragged on an interminable course."

This " new power in history "—the ability of one man to alter human civilization—began with Genghis Khan and ended with his grandson Kubilai, when the Mongol empire tended to break up. It has not reappeared since.

In this volume no effort has been made to apologize for, or further to drench with blood, the character of Genghis Khan. Allowance has been made for the fact that most of our knowledge of the conqueror has been based, in the past, upon the accounts given by medieval Europeans, Persians and Syrians, who with the Chinese proper were the greatest victims of Mongol destructiveness. Cæsar wrote his own memoirs of the Gallic conquest, and Alexander had his Arrian and Quintus Curtius.

We find in Genghis Khan—when we look at the man in his own environment—a ruler who did not put to death any of his sons, ministers or generals. Both Juchi and Kassar, his brother, gave him some occasion for cruelty, and he might have been expected to execute the Mongol officers who allowed themselves to be defeated. Ambassadors from all peoples came to him and returned safely. Nor do we find that he tortured captives except in unusual circumstances.

The warlike and kindred nations, the Karaïts, Ugurs, and *Liao-tung*—the Men of Iron—were dealt with leniently, as were the Armenians, Georgians and the remnants of the crusaders by his descendants. Genghis Khan was careful to preserve what he thought might be useful to himself and his people; the rest was destroyed. As he advanced farther from his homeland, into strange civilizations, this destruction became almost universal.

We moderns are beginning to understand how this unprecedented annihilation of human life and works earned for him the vituperation of Mohammedans. Just as his unexampled genius gained for him the veneration of his Buddhists.

Because Genghis Khan did not, like Mohammed the prophet, make war on the world for a religion, or —like Alexander and Napoleon—for personal and political aggrandizement, we have been mystified. The explanation of the mystery lies in the primitive simplicity of the Mongol's character.

He took from the world what he wanted for his sons and his people. He did this by war, because he knew no other means. What he did not want he destroyed, because he did not know what else to do with it.

II

IN the middle of the twelfth century reports reached Europe of the victories of a Christian monarch of Asia over the Turks—" *Iohannes Presbyter Rex Armeniæ et Indiæ.*" Latter-day research assures us that this first inkling of a Christian king east of Jerusalem came from tidings of victories gained over the Mohammedans by John, High Constable of Georgia, in the Caucasus—a region then vaguely associated with both Armenia and India.

It was recalled that the three Magi had emerged from this region ; the crusading spirit flamed in Europe and stories of an all-powerful Christian potentate in far Asia gained greatly in the telling. The Nestorian Christians, scattered from Armenia to Cathay, saw fit to indite and send to the Pope Alexander III a letter purporting to be from Prester John describing vast splendour and many wonders in the medieval manner—processions over the desert, an *entourage* of seventy kings, fabulous beasts, a city upon the sands. In short a pretty good summary of the myths of the day.

But so far as there existed truth in the description, it fitted Wang Khan (pronounced by the Nestorians Ung Khan, or " King John ") of the Karaïts, who were largely Christians. His city of Karakorum might be termed the stronghold of the long-neglected Nestorians of Asia. It was a desert city, and he was an emperor, having khans or kings for subjects. Various chronicles mention the conversion of a king of the " Keriths." Marco Polo found in Wang Khan the actor of the shadowy *rôle* of Prester John.*

* See Yule Cordier, *Travels of Marco Polo,* I, 230-237. Also Baring-Gould's *Myths of the Middle Ages.*

III

1. " It is ordered to believe that there is only one God, creator of heaven and earth, who alone gives life and death, riches and poverty as pleases Him—and who has over everything an absolute power.

2. Leaders of a religion, preachers, monks, persons who are dedicated to religious practice, the criers of mosques, physicians and those who bathe the bodies of the dead are to be freed from public charges.

3. It is forbidden under penalty of death that anyone, whoever he be, shall be proclaimed emperor unless he has been elected previously by the princes, khans, officers and other Mongol nobles in a general council.

4. It is forbidden chieftains of nations and clans subject to the Mongols to hold honorary titles.

5. Forbidden ever to make peace with a monarch, a prince or a people who have not submitted.

6. The ruling that divides men of the army into tens, hundreds, thousands, and ten thousands is to be maintained. This arrangement serves to raise an army in a short time, and to form the units of commands.

7. The moment a campaign begins, each soldier must receive his arms from the hand of the officer who has them in charge. The soldier must keep them in

good order, and have them inspected by his officer before a battle.

8. Forbidden, under death penalty, to pillage the enemy before the general commanding gives permission ; but after this permission is given the soldier must have the same opportunity as the officer, and must be allowed to keep what he has carried off, provided he has paid his share to the receiver for the emperor.

9. To keep the men of the army exercised, a great hunt shall be held every winter. On this account, it is forbidden any man of the empire to kill between the months of March and October, deer, bucks, roebucks, hares, wild ass and some birds.

10. Forbidden, to cut the throats of animals slain for food ; they must be bound, the chest opened and the heart pulled out by the hand of the hunter.

11. It is permitted to eat the blood and entrails of animals—though this was forbidden before now.

12. (A list of privileges and immunities assured to the chieftains and officers of the new empire.)

13. Every man who does not go to war must work for the empire, without reward, for a certain time.

14. Men guilty of the theft of a horse or steer or a thing of equal value will be punished by death and their bodies cut into two parts. For lesser thefts the punishment shall be, according to the value of the thing stolen, a number of blows of a staff—seven, seventeen, twenty-seven, up to seven hundred. But this bodily punishment may be avoided by paying nine times the worth of the thing stolen.

15. No subject of the empire may take a Mongol for servant or slave. Every man, except in rare cases, must join the army.

16. To prevent the flight of alien slaves, it is forbidden to give them asylum, food or clothing, under pain of death. Any man who meets an escaped slave and does not bring him back to his master will be punished in the same manner.

17. The law of marriage orders that every man shall purchase his wife, and that marriage between the first and second degrees of kinship is forbidden. A man may marry two sisters, or have several concubines. The women should attend to the care of property, buying and selling at their pleasure. Men should occupy themselves only with hunting and war. Children born of slaves are legitimate as the children of wives. The offspring of the first woman shall be honoured above other children and shall inherit everything.

18. Adultery is to be punished by death, and those guilty of it may be slain out of hand.

19. If two families wish to be united by marriage and have only young children, the marriage of these children is allowed, if one be a boy and the other a girl. If the children are dead, the marriage contract may still be drawn up.

20. It is forbidden to bathe or wash garments in running water during thunder.

21. Spies, false witnesses, all men given to infamous vices, and sorcerers are condemned to death.

22. Officers and chieftains who fail in their duty, or do not come at the summons of the Khan are to be slain, especially in remote districts. If their offence be less grave, they must come in person before the Khan."

These examples of the laws of Genghis Khan are

translated from Pétis de la Croix, who explains that
he has not been able to come upon a complete list of
the laws—a "*Yassa Gengizcani*." He has gleaned
these twenty-two rulings from various sources, the
Persian chroniclers, and Fras Rubruquis and Carpini.
The list given is palpably incomplete, and has come
down to us from alien sources.

The explanation of the curious tenth law may
probably be found in existing religious prejudices as
to the manner of killing game to be eaten. The
eleventh rule seems to aim at preserving a possible
source of food in time of famine. The twentieth law
concerning water and thunder is explained by
Rubruquis—to prevent the Mongols, who were very
much afraid of thunder, from throwing themselves
into lakes and rivers during a storm.

Pétis de la Croix says that the *Yassa* of Genghis
Khan was followed by Timur-i-lang. Babar, the first
of the Moghuls (Mongols) of India, says: "My
forefathers and family had always sacredly observed
the rules of Chengiz. In their parties, their courts,
their festivals and their entertainments, in their
sitting down and rising up, they never acted contrary
to the institutions of Chengiz."—*Memoirs of Babar,
Emperor of Hindustan*—Erskine and Leyden edition,
1826, p. 202.

IV

IT is a common and quite natural mistake among historians to describe the Mongol army as a vast multitude. Even Dr. Stanley Lane-Poole, one of the most distinguished of modern authorities, cannot resist the inevitable *bi nehaiet* and speaks of " Chingkiz Khan followed by hordes of nomads like the sands of the sea without number."—*Turkey* (Stories of the Nations).

In our understanding of the Mongols we have advanced sufficiently far beyond the ideas of Matthew Paris and the medieval monks to be certain that the horde of Genghis Khan was not, like the Huns, a migratory mass, but a disciplined army of invasion. The *personnel* of the horde is given by Sir Henry Howorth as follows :

Imperial Guards	..	..	..	..	1,000
The Centre, under Tuli	..	..	..	101,000
Right Wing	..	..	..	..	47,000
Left Wing	..	..	..	..	52,000
Other Contingents	..	..	..	29,000

230,000

This is apparently the strength of the army at the time of the war against the Shah and the west. It is, therefore, the largest assembled by Genghis Khan.

The other contingents consisted of the 10,000 Cathayans, and the forces of the Idikut of the Ugurs, and the Khan of Almalyk—the last two being sent back after the invasion began.

The brilliant scholar, Léon Cahun, maintains that an army of Mongol effectives did not number over 30,000. There being three such army corps in this campaign—besides Juchi's 20,000 and the allies—the host would amount to some 150,000 warriors by this calculation. And certainly no greater numbers could have existed for a winter in the barren valleys of high Asia.

The army commanded by Genghis Khan at the time of his death is known to have consisted of four corps with the imperial guard—some 130,000 men. Turning to the scanty figures available as to the populations of the Gobi lands, we can approximate the total at no more than 1,500,000 souls. From this number no more than 200,000 effectives could very well be mustered. Brigadier-General Sir Percy Sykes, in his *Persia*, comments on the " Mongols who were numerically weak and fought thousands of miles from their base."

Contemporary Mohammedan chroniclers habitually exaggerated the numbers of the horde, mentioning five hundred to eight hundred thousand. But all available evidence indicates that Genghis Khan performed during the years 1219-1225, the remarkable military feat of subjecting the country from Tibet to the Caspian sea, with no more than 100,000 men— and from the Dnieper to the China sea with no more than 250,000, in all. And of this number probably not more than half were Mongols. The chronicles mention 50,000 Turkoman allies at the end of the campaigns ; Juchi's forces were augmented by throngs of the wild Kipchak, the Desert People.   In China the ancestors of the present-day Koreans and Manchus were fighting under the Mongol standards.

In the reign of Ogotai, the son of Genghis Khan, more Turkish tribes of mid-Asia joined the Mongols, who gave them their fill of fighting.   These made up the greater part of the army with which Subotai and Batu conquered eastern Europe.   Certainly, Ogotai had more than half a million effective fighting men in his armies, and Mangu and Kubilai, grand-sons of Genghis Khan, double that number.

V

THE MONGOL PLAN OF INVASION

THE horde of Genghis Khan followed a fixed plan in invading a hostile country. This method met with unvarying success until the Mongols were checked by the Mamluks in their advance upon Egypt across the Syrian desert about 1270.

1. A *kurultai*, or general council, was summoned at the headquarters of the Kha Khan. All higher officers except those given permission to remain on active service were expected to attend the council. Here the situation was discussed, and the plan of the campaign explained. Routes were selected, and the various divisions chosen for service.

2. Spies were sent out, and informers brought in to be questioned.

3. The doomed country was entered from several points at once. The separate divisions or army corps each had its general commanding, who moved toward a fixed objective. He was at liberty to manœuvre, and to engage the enemy at his discretion, but must keep in touch by courier with headquarters—the Khan or Orkhon.

4. The separate divisions posted corps of observation before the larger fortified towns, while the neighbouring district was ravaged. Supplies were gathered off the country and a temporary base estab-

lished if the campaign was to be a long one. Seldom
did the Mongols merely screen a strong city ; they
were more apt to invest it—a *tuman* or two remaining
behind with captives and engines for siege work,
while the main force moved on.

When faced by a hostile army in the field, the
Mongols followed one of two courses. If possible,
they surprised the enemy by a rapid march of a day
and a night—two or more Mongol divisions concen-
trating at the place of battle at a given hour, as in
disposing of the Hungarians near Pesth in 1241.
If this did not succeed, the enemy would be surrounded,
or the Mongols would envelop one flank, in the swift
tulughma, or "standard sweep."

Other expedients were to feign flight and withdraw for several days until the hostile forces became
scattered or off their guard. Then the Mongols
would mount fresh horses and turn to attack. This
manœuvre brought disaster to the powerful Russian
host near the Dnieper.

Often in this deceptive retreat they would extend
their line until the enemy was surrounded without
realizing it. If the hostile troops massed together
and fought bravely, the Mongol enveloping line
would open, allowing them to retreat. They would
then be attacked on the march. This was the fate of
the Bokharan army.

Many of these expedients were practised by the
resourceful early Turks, the Hiung-nu, from whom
the Mongols themselves were in part descended. The
Cathayans were accustomed to manœuvre in cavalry
columns, and the Chinese proper knew all the rules of
strategy. It remained for Genghis Khan to supply

the inflexible purpose and the rare ability to do the right thing at the right time—and to hold his men under iron restraint.

" Even the Chinese said that he led his armies like a god. The manner in which he moved large bodies of men over vast distances without an apparent effort, the judgment he showed in the conduct of several wars in countries far apart from each other, his strategy in unknown regions, always on the alert yet never allowing hesitation or overcaution to interfere with his enterprises, the sieges he brought to a successful termination, his brilliant victories, a succession of ' suns of Austerlitz,' all combined, make up the picture of a career to which Europe can offer nothing that will surpass, if indeed she has anything to bear comparison with it "—so Demetrius Boulger sums up the military genius of the great Mongol. (*A Short History of China*, p. 100.)

VI

WE have very little accurate knowledge of any of the Chinese inventions before Genghis Khan and his Mongols opened up the road into that much secluded empire. After then, that is after 1211, we hear of gunpowder frequently. It was used in the *ho-pao* or fire-projectors.

In one siege the *ho-pao* are mentioned as burning and destroying wooden towers. The discharge of the powder in the fire projectors made " a noise like thunder, heard at a distance of a hundred *li*." This means about thirty miles, but is probably an exaggeration. At the siege of Kaifong in 1232 a Chinese annalist records the following : "As the Mongols had dug themselves pits under the earth where they were sheltered from missiles, we decided to bind with iron the machines called *chin-tien-lei* (a kind of fire-projector) and lowered them into the places where the Mongol sappers were ; they exploded and blew into pieces men and shields."

Again, in the time of Kubilai Khan : " The Emperor . . . ordered a fire gun to be discharged ; the report caused a panic among the (enemy) troops."

Dr. Herbert Gowen of the University of Washington points out a Japanese reference to these Mongol weapons, taken from a fourteenth century source.

"Iron balls, like footballs, were let fly with a sound like cartwheels rolling down a steep declivity, and accompanied by flashes like lightning."

It is clear that the Chinese and Mongols knew the detonating effect of gunpowder ; it is also clear that their fire-projectors were used chiefly to burn or frighten the enemy. They did not know how to cast cannon, and made little progress with projectiles, depending still on the massive torsion and counter-weight siege engines.

Now these same Mongols overran central Europe in 1238-40 and were still in what is now Russian Poland or Polish Russia during the lifetime of the monk Schwartz. Freiburg was well within the area of their conquest, and the German monk must have worked at his inventions within some three hundred miles of a Mongol garrison. (In justice to Schwartz's claim one must add that there is no established record of the Mongols using powder in Europe. But it must be remembered that merchants were constantly dealing with them and passing back into the European cities.)

Turning to Friar Roger Bacon, we find that he did not, it seems, produce any gunpowder for public use himself. He recorded the existence of such a compound, and its fulminating qualities. Roger Bacon met, talked with and availed himself of the geographical and other knowledge gained by Friar William of Rubruk, who was sent by St. Louis of France as envoy to the Mongols. The *Opus Majus* of Roger Bacon says concerning the book of William of Rubruk " which book I have seen, and with its author I have talked." (Against this it can be argued

P

that Rubruk's book makes no mention of gunpowder, and that we cannot assume he became
acquainted with it during his half-year's sojourn at
the Mongol court, while Bacon's first mention of the
specific ingredients of powder—that is, of saltpetre
and sulphur—ante-dates slightly Rubruk's return
from his journey.)

It is a matter purely of individual opinion how
much weight one chooses to give to the circumstance
that the two ostensible inventors of gunpowder in
Europe both lived during the seventy-five odd years
when Europe was aroused by the Mongol invasions,
and the weapons used by the invaders, and both had
contact of sorts with the Mongols.

But there is indisputable evidence that *fire-arms*
and cannon both began to appear in Germany about
the time of the Monk Schwartz. Cannon were
improved and developed rapidly in Europe and
entered Asia by way of Constantinople and the Turks.
Thus we find Babar, the first of the Moghuls, equipped
with large bore-cannon, handled by Roumis (Turks)
in 1525. And the first metal cannon were cast in
China by Jesuits in the seventeenth century.

And—a curious picture it is—we see the European
Cossacks, invading the dominion of the Tartars in
1581 with serviceable muskets, while the men of
Asia dragged out an unloaded cannon, ignorant of
its use, expecting it to blast the invaders.

To sum up : The Chinese made gunpowder and
understood its explosive qualities long before Friars
Bacon and Schwartz, but put it to little use in warfare.
Whether the Europeans learned about it from them
or discovered it on their own account is an open

question ; but Europeans certainly made the first
serviceable cannon.

The truth, probably, will never be known. It is
curious that Matthew Paris and Thomas of Spalato
and other medieval chroniclers speak of the fear
inspired by the Mongols who carried with them smoke
and flame into battle. This might be an allusion to
the trick often practised by the troopers of the Gobi,
of setting fire to the dry grass of a countryside and
advancing behind the flames. But very probably
this may indicate the use of gunpowder—which was
not yet known in Europe—by the Mongols, in their
fire pots. Carpini has a curious reference to a species
of flame thrower used by the Mongol horsemen, and
fanned by some kind of bellows.

At all events, this apparition of flame and smoke
among the Mongols was accepted by our medieval
chroniclers as certain indication that they were demons.

VII

THE CONJURERS AND THE CROSS

WHEN the Mongol divisions under Subotai and Chepé Noyon were forcing their way through the Caucasus they encountered and defeated an army of Christian Georgians. Rusudan, queen of the Georgians, sent to the Pope a letter by David, bishop of Ani, in which she stated that the Mongols had displayed before their ranks a standard bearing the Cross and that this had deceived the Georgians into thinking that the Mongols were Christians.

Again at the battle of Liegnitz, the Polish chroniclers relate that the Mongols appeared with "a great standard bearing an emblem like the Greek letter X." One historian observes that this might have been a device of the *shamans* to ridicule the Cross, and the emblem might have been formed by the crossed thigh-bones of a sheep, used frequently by the *shamans* in divination. It was rendered terrifying by the clouds of smoke that eddied up from the pots carried by the long-robed attendants of the standard.

It is not likely that military leaders as intelligent as the Mongol Orkhons would endeavour to deceive an enemy by carrying a cross before them. It is possible that Nestorian Christians in the Mongol army might have marched with the Cross, and that priests were seen accompanying it at Liegnitz and perhaps carrying censers.

VIII

THE test of strength between Mongol and European did not come during the lifetime of Genghis Khan. It followed the great council of 1235, in the Khanship of Ogotai.

Briefly, this is what happened :

Batu, the son of Juchi, marched west with the Golden Horde to take possession of the lands galloped over by Subotai in 1223. From 1238 to the autumn of 1240 Batu, the " Splendid," overran the Volga clans, Russian cities and the steppes of the Black Sea, finally storming Kiev and sending raiding columns into southern Poland, or rather Ruthenia, since Poland was then divided into a number of principalities.

When the snows melted in March, 1241, the Mongol headquarters was north of the Carpathians between modern Lemberg and Kiev. Subotai, the directing genius of the campaign, was confronted by the following enemies :

In front of him Boleslas the Chaste, overlord of Poland, had assembled his host. Beyond, to the north, in Silesia, Henry the Pious was gathering an army 30,000 strong of Poles, Bavarians, Teutonic Knights and Templars out of France, who had volunteered to repel this invasion of barbarians. A hundred miles or so behind Boleslas, the king of Bohemia was mobilizing a still stronger army, receiving contingents from Austria, Saxony and Brandenburg.

On the left front of the Mongols, Mieceslas of Galicia and other lords were preparing to defend their lands in the Carpathians. On the Mongol left, farther away, the Magyar host of Hungary, a hundred thousand strong, was mustering under the banner of Bela IV, the king, beyond the Carpathian mountains.

If Batu and Subotai turned south into Hungary, they would have left the Polish army at their rear ; if they advanced due west, to meet the Poles, the Hungarians would be on their flank.

Subotai and Batu seem to have been perfectly well aware of the preparations of the Christian hosts. Their scouting expeditions of the previous year had brought them valuable information about the country and the monarchs opposed to them. On the other hand, the Christian kings had little knowledge of the movements of the Mongols.

Batu acted as soon as the ground was dry enough for his horses to move over—in spite of the marshes along the Pripet and the damp forests that fringed the Carpathian ranges. He divided his host into four army corps, sending the strongest, under two reliable generals, grandsons of Genghis Khan, Kaidu and Baibars, against the Poles.

This division moved rapidly west and encountered the forces of Boleslas as the Poles were pursuing some scouting contingents of Mongols. The Poles attacked with their usual bravery and were defeated—Boleslas fleeing into Moravia and the remnants of his men withdrawing to the north, whither the Mongols did not pursue them. This was March 18. Cracov was

burned, and the Mongols of Kaidu and Baibars
hastened on to meet the Duke of Silesia before he
could join forces with the Bohemians.

They encountered this army of Henry the Pious
near Liegnitz, April 9. Of the battle that followed
we have no first-hand account. We only know that
the German and Polish forces broke before the onset
of the Mongol-standard, and were almost exterminated;
Henry and his barons died to a man, as did the
Hospitallers. It is said that the grand master of the
Teutonic Knights perished on the field, with nine
Templars and five hundred men-at-arms.[*]

Liegnitz was burned by its defenders, and the day
after the battle Kaidu and Baibars and their division
confronted the larger army of Wenceslas, king of
Bohemia, fifty miles away. Wenceslas moved slowly
from place to place, as the Mongols appeared and
disappeared. His cumbersome array, too strong to be
attacked by the Mongol division, could not come up
with the horsemen from Cathay, who rested their
mounts and ravaged Silesia and beautiful Moravia
under his eyes, and finally tricked Wenceslas into
marching north while they turned south to rejoin
Batu.

"And know," Ponce d'Aubon wrote to St. Louis
of France, "that all the barons of Germany and the
king, and all the clergy and those in Hungary have
taken the Cross to go against the Tatars. And, if

---

[*] "Tartarin ont la terre qui fu Henri le duc de Poulainne destruite et
escillie, et celui meismes ocis avec mout des barons, et six de nos frères et
trois chevaliers et deux sergans et 500 de nos hommes ont mort."—Letter
of the Grand Master of the French Templars to Saint Louis, quoted by Léon
Cahun.

Legend has it that the Mongols cut an ear from every dead enemy
and filled in this manner nine sacks that they carried back to Batu, their
prince. The head of the unfortunate Henry was carried on a lance to Liegnitz.

what our brothers have told us is true, if it happens
by the will of God that they be vanquished, these
Tatars will not find anyone to stand against them as
far as your land."

But when the Master of the Templars wrote this,
the Hungarian host was already vanquished. Subotai
and Batu threaded through the Carpathians in three
divisions, the right flank entering Hungary from
Galicia, the left, under command of Subotai, swinging
down through Moldavia. The smaller armies in their
path were wiped out, and the three columns joined
forces before Bela and his Hungarians near Pesth.

It was then the beginning of April, just before the
battle of Liegnitz. Subotai and Batu had not heard
how matters were going in the north ; they dispatched
a division to open communication with the grandsons
of Genghis Khan on the Oder.

The small army of the bishop of Ugolin advanced
against them ; they retreated to a marshy region and
surrounded the rash Hungarians. The bishop fled
with three companions, sole survivors.

Meanwhile Bela began to cross the Danube with
his host—Magyars, Croats and Germans, with the
French Templars who had been posted in Hungary.
A hundred thousand in all. The Mongols retreated
slowly before them, at a hand pace. Batu, Subotai,
Mangu—conqueror of Kiev—had left the army and
were inspecting the site chosen for the battle. This
was the plain of Mohi, hemmed in on four sides, by
the river Sayo, by the vine-clad hills of Tokay, by
" dark woods and the great hills of Lomnitz."

The - Mongols retreated across the river, leaving
intact a wide stone bridge, and pushing into the

brush on the far side for some five miles. Blindly the host of Bela followed, and *camped in the plain of Mohi*. Camped with its heavy baggage, its sergeants-at-arms, its mailed chivalry and followers. A thousand men were posted on the far side of the bridge, and explored the woods without seeing a sign of the enemy.

Night. Subotai took command of the Mongol right, led it in a wide circle back to the river where he had observed a ford. He set to work building a bridge to aid in the crossing.

The break of dawn. Batu's advance moved back toward the bridge, surprised and annihilated the detachment guarding it. His main forces were thrown across, seven catapults playing on Bela's knights who tried to stem the rush of horsemen across the bridge. The Mongols surged steadily into the disordered array of their foes, the terrible standard with its nine yak-tails surrounded by the smoke of fires carried in pans by *shamans*. "A great grey face with a long beard," one of the Europeans described it, "giving out noisome smoke."

No doubting the bravery of Bela's paladins. The battle was stubborn and unbroken until near midday. Then Subotai finished his flank movement, and appeared behind Bela's array. The Mongols charged in, broke the Hungarians. Like the Teutonic Knights at Liegnitz, the Templars died to a man on the field.*

Then the Mongol ranks parted in the west, leaving open the road through the gorge by which the host of Bela had advanced to the plain. The Hungarians fled, and were pursued at leisure. For two days' journey

---

* " *Magister vero Templarius cum tota acie Latinorum occubuit.*"—Thomas de Spalato, cited by Léon Cahun.

the bodies of Europeans strewed the roads. Forty thousand had fallen. Bela separated from his remaining followers, leaving his brother dying, the Archbishop slain. By sheer speed of his horse he freed himself from the pursuit, hid along the bank of the Danube, was hunted out and fled into the Carpathians. There, in time, he reached the same monastery that sheltered his brother-monarch of Poland, Boleslas the Chaste.

The Mongols stormed Pesth, and fired the suburbs of Gran. They advanced into Austria as far as Nieustadt, avoided the sluggish host of Germans and Bohemians, and turned down to the Adriatic, ravaging the towns along the coast except Ragusa. In less than two months they had overrun Europe from the headwaters of the Elbe to the sea, had defeated three great armies and a dozen smaller ones and had taken by assault all the towns except Olmutz which made good its defence under Yaroslav of Sternberg with twelve thousand men.

No second Tours saved western Europe from inevitable disaster.* Its armies, capable only of moving in a mass, led by reigning monarchs as incompetent as Bela or Saint Louis of France, were valiant enough but utterly unable to prevail against the rapidly manœuvring Mongols led by generals such as Subotai and Mangu and Kaidu—veterans of a lifetime of war on two continents. But the war never came to a final issue. A courier from Karakorum brought the Mongols

---

* A summary of this campaign—which has been much discussed and little understood—can be found in Henri Cordier's *Mélanges d'Histoire et de Géographie Orientales*, Tome II , also in Sir Henry Howorth's *History of the Mongols*, Vol I. Fuller details are given in Léon Cahun's *Introduction à L'Histoire de L'Asie*, pp 3[.]9-374 and in *Der Einfall der Mongolen in Mittel Europa* by Strakosch Grassmann.

the tidings of Ogotai's death and a summons to return
to the Gobi.

At the council there a year later, the battle of Mohi
had a curious aftermath. Batu accused Subotai of
being tardy in arriving on the field and causing the
loss of many Mongols. The old general made answer
tartly :

"Remember that the river was not deep before
thee, and a bridge was already there. Where I crossed,
the river was deep and I had to build a bridge."

Batu admitted the truth of this, and did not blame
Subotai again.

WHAT EUROPE THOUGHT OF THE MONGOLS

ENOUGH, perhaps, has been said here to show that the Mongol armies possessed several advantages over the Europeans of that day. They were more mobile—Subotai rode with his division two hundred and ninety miles in less than three days during the invasion of Hungary. The same Ponce d'Aubon makes the comment that the Mongols could march in a single day as far " as from Chartres to Paris."

" No people in the world," asserts a contemporary chronicler of Europe,* speaking of the Mongols, " is as able—especially in conflicts in open country—in defeating an enemy either by personal bravery, or by knowledge of warfare."

This opinion is confirmed by Fra Carpini, who was sent to the Mongol Khan not long after the terrible invasion of 1238-1242, to exhort the pagan conquerors to cease the slaughter of Christian peoples. " No single kingdom or province can resist the Tartars." And he adds : " The Tartars fight more by stratagem than by sheer force."

This daring priest—who seems to have had an eye for things military—remarks that the " Tartars " were less numerous and lacked the physical stature and strength of the Europeans. And he goes on to urge European monarchs—who always took command of

* Thomas de Spalato, cited by Léon Cahun.

their hosts in a war, no matter how lacking they might be in the qualifications of such leadership—to model their military system on the Mongol.

" Our armies ought to be marshalled after the order of the Tartars, and under the same rigorous laws of war. The field of battle ought to be chosen, if possible, in a plain where everything is visible on all sides. The army should by no means be drawn up in one body, but in many divisions. Scouts ought to be sent out on every side. Our generals ought to keep their troops day and night on the alert, and always armed, ready for battle ; as the Tartars are always vigilant as devils.

" If the princes and rulers of Christendom mean to resist their progress, it is requisite that they should make common cause and oppose them with united council."

Carpini did not fail to notice the weapons of the Mongols and advised the European soldiery to improve their arms. " The princes of Christendom ought to have many soldiers armed with strong-bows, cross-bows and artillery which the Tartars dread. Besides these, there ought to be men armed with good iron maces, or with axes having long handles. The steel arrow-heads should be tempered in the Tartar manner by being plunged, while hot, into water mixed with salt, that they may be better able to penetrate armour. Our men ought to have good helmets and armour of proof for themselves and horses. And those who are not so armed, ought to keep in the rear of those who are."

Carpini had received a vivid impression of the devastating archery of the Mongol children of war. " Men and horses they wound and slay with arrows, and when men and mounts are shattered in this fashion, they then close in upon them."

At this time the Emperor Frederick II—the same who waged the famous feud with the Pope—called for aid from the other princes, and wrote to the king of England : " The Tartars are men of small stature but sturdy limbs—high-strung, valiant and daring, always ready to throw themselves into peril at a sign from their commander. . . . But—and this we cannot say without sighing—formerly they were covered with leather and armour of iron plates, while now they are equipped with finer and more useful armour, the spoils taken from Christians, so that we may be shamefully and dolorously slain with our own weapons. Moreover, they are mounted on better horses, they sustain themselves on choicer foods and wear garments less rude than our own."

About the time that he wrote this the Emperor Frederick was summoned by the victorious Mongol army of invasion to become a subject of the Great Khan. The terms offered were fair from the Mongol point of view—for the Emperor to yield himself and his people captive, so that their lives might be spared,* and go himself to Karakorum and there occupy himself with whatever official post might be selected for him. To this Frederick answered good-naturedly that he knew enough about birds of prey to qualify as the Khan's falconer.

* " Il fallait reconnaître leur empire ou mourir "—Abel Rémusat. Submission involved paying a heavy tax, which was sometimes collected two or three times over The Mongols were both tolerant and rapacious
One cannot read the annals of Genghis Khan without realizing that he never moved to war without good occasion to do so. One suspects that he often created the occasion himself, but it was, nevertheless, created. He instilled into his victorious Mongols three ideas that persisted for generations —that they must not destroy peoples who submitted voluntarily, that they must never cease from war with those who resisted, and that they must tolerate all religions in equal measure.

X

CORRESPONDENCE BETWEEN THE EUROPEAN MONARCHS AND THE MONGOLS

AFTER Batu and Subotai withdrew from Europe in 1242, a widespread dread of another Mongol invasion impelled the sovereigns of Christendom to action in various ways. Innocent IV called the Council of Lyons to discuss, among other matters, some safeguard for Christianity. Heedless St. Louis declared that if the " Tartars " appeared again, the chivalry of France would die in the defence of the Church. Whereupon, he started off on the disastrous crusades into Egypt, sending at various times priests and messages to the Mongols south of the Caspian, commanded at that time by Baichu Khan.

One of his embassies was forwarded to the Khan at Karakorum with an amusing result. Joinville, a medieval chronicler, tells us that when the envoys were presented with their slight gifts, the Khan turned to the nobles gathered around him and said, " Lords, here is the submission of the King of the Franks, and here is the tribute he has sent us."

The Mongols frequently urged Louis to make submission to their Khan, to give tribute and be protected as other rulers were, by the power of the Khan. They advised also, that he make war on the Seljuks in Asia Minor, with whom they were then engaged. Louis some years later sent the lusty and intelligent Rubruquis to the court of the Khan, but was careful to instruct the monk not to present himself as an envoy, or to let his journey be construed as an act of subjection.

Among the letters that reached Louis from the horde was one mentioning the fact that many Christians were to be found among the Mongols. "We have come with authority and power to announce that all Christians are to be freed from servitude and taxes in Mohammedan lands, and are to be treated with honour and reverence. No one is to molest their goods and those of their churches which have been destroyed are to be rebuilt and are to be allowed to sound their plates." *

It is true that there were several Christian wives of the Mongol Il-khans of Persia, and that Christian Armenians served them as ministers. Remnants of the crusaders abandoned in Palestine fought at times in the Mongol ranks. And the Il-khan Arghun did rebuild churches that had been destroyed in the previous wars.

And an angered Mohammedan wrote that in the year 1259 the Mongol Il-khan Hulagu commanded that, in the whole of Syria, "every religious sect should proclaim its faith openly, and that no Moslem should disapprove. On that day there was no single Christian of the common people or of the highest who did not put on his finest apparel." *†

Whatever may have been their leaning toward the Christians in Palestine, the Mongol leaders did

* Howorth, *History of the Mongols*, Part III.
*† *An Answer to the Dhimmis*—Richard Gottheil, " Journal of the American Oriental Society," Dec., 1921.

sincerely desire the aid of European armies against the Mohammedans, and in 1274 sent an embassy of sixteen men to the Pope, and then to Edward I of England who answered with a good deal of casuistry —since he had no intention of faring toward Jerusalem: " We note the resolution you have taken to relieve the Holy Land from the enemies of Christianity. This is most grateful to us, and we thank you. But we cannot at present send you any certain news about the time of our arrival in the Holy Land."

Meanwhile, the Pope sent other envoys to Baichu, near the Caspian. These offended the Mongols very much, because they did not know the name of the Khan and because they lectured the pagans on the sin of shedding blood. The Mongols said that the Pope must be very ignorant if he did not know the name of the man who ruled all the world, and as for slaughtering their enemies, they did that at the command of the son of Heaven himself. Baichu was minded to execute the unfortunate priests, but spared them and sent them back safely because they were, after all, envoys.

The reply of Baichu, given in a letter to these emissaries of Innocent IV, is worth quoting :

" By order of the supreme Khan, Baichu Noyon sends these words—Pope, dost thou know that thine envoys have come to us with thy letters ? Thine envoys have uttered big words. We know not whether they did so by thine order. So, we send thee this message. If thou desirest to reign over the land and water, thy patrimony, thou must come thyself, Pope, to us, and present thyself before him who reigns over the surface of all the earth. And if thou

Q

comest not, we know not what will happen. God knows. Only, it would be well to send messengers to say whether thou wilt come or no, and whether thou wilt come in friendship or no." *

Needless to say, Innocent IV did not make the journey to Karakorum. Nor did the Mongols return again to middle Europe. But there is no indication that the armed chivalry of western Europe restrained them. At Nieustadt in Austria they had advanced nearly six thousand miles from their homeland. Subotai and the fierce Tuli died. Batu, the son of Juchi, was well content with Sari, his golden city on the Volga. Civil war smouldered along the wastes of Asia, and the westward march of the hordes came to an end. They ravaged Hungary again near the close of the thirteenth century, then retired to the plains of the Volga.

---

* From the *Speculum Historiale* of Vincent de Beauvais   In this letter appears again the ominous phrase, " We know not what will happen. God knows "   the usual phrase of warning when the Mongols meant war   To the Seljuk prince, Kai Kosru, they returned a laconic answer   " Thou hast spoken bravely. God will give victory as He pleases"   It seems that they always sent envoys to an enemy, after the custom of Genghis Khan, offering terms. If these were refused, they uttered their warning and made ready for war.

THE TOMB OF GENGHIS KHAN

THE story printed in a London newspaper that Professor Peter Kozloff had found and identified the burial place of the Mongol conqueror excited great interest recently. This report was later denied by Professor Lozloff, according to a cable from Leningrad printed in the *New York Times*, November 11th, 1927.

Professor Kozloff in relating the results of his last trip to the site of Kara Khoto in the southern Gobi during 1925-26, and the evidences of early Scythian-Siberian culture found there, pointed out that the site of the sepulchre of Genghis Khan is still unknown.

There exist many conflicting traditions as to this vanished sepulchre. Marco Polo mentions it vaguely, assuming it to be among the tombs of the later Mongol sovereigns.

Rashid el-Din says that Genghis Khan was buried at a hill called Yakka Kuruk near Urga, a place frequently mentioned by Ssanang Setzen. Quatremere and others go to some lengths to identify this hill with the Khanula near Urga. But all this is doubtful.

The Archimandrite Palladius says: " There are no accurate indications in the documents of the Mongol period on the burial place of Chingiz Khan."

243

A more modern tradition, cited by E. T. C. Werner, places the tomb of the conqueror in the Ordos country, at Etjen Koro. Here, on the twenty-first day of the third month a ceremony is attended on this site by Mongol princes. Relics of the great Khan, a saddle, a bow and other things, are brought to the burial site, which is not a tomb but an encampment, walled in by piled stone. Here stand two white felt tents containing, it is believed, a casket of stone. What is in the casket is unknown.

Mr. Werner believes that the Mongols are correct in saying that the remains of the conqueror may lie in this encampment, still guarded by five hundred families who still have special rights. It is situated beyond the great wall, south of the loop of the Hoang, about 40 N. Lat. and 109 E. Long.

In evidence of this, he quotes the statement of the Mongol prince of Kalachin, a descendant of Genghis Khan. And this, perhaps, is better evidence than the vague and conflicting accounts of the chronicles.

For further details, consult the Yule-Cordier 1903 edition of *Marco Polo*, Vol. I, pp. 247-251, also *The Tomb of Marco Polo*, by E. T. C. Werner; and W. W. Rockhill's Diary.

XII

FEW men have had a more difficult part to play in life than this young Cathayan who caught the eye of Genghis Khan. He was one of the first Chinese philosophers to ride with the horde, and the Mongols did not make matters easy for the student of philosophy and astronomy and medicine. An officer who was noted for his skill as a maker of bows chaffed the tall and long-bearded Cathayan :

" What business has a man of books," he asked, " among a fellowship of warriors ? "

" To make fine bows," Ye Liu Chutsai replied, " a wood worker is needed ; but when it comes to governing an empire, a man of wisdom is needed."

He became a favourite of the old conqueror and during the long march into the west, while the other Mongols were gathering rich spoil, the Cathayan collected books and astronomical tables and herbs for his own use. He noted down the geography of the march, and when an epidemic seized the horde, he enjoyed a philosopher's revenge on the officers who had made sport of him. He dosed them with rhubarb and cured them.

Genghis Khan valued him for his integrity, and Ye Liu Chutsai lost no opportunity to check the slaughter that marked the path of the horde. There is a legend that in the defiles of the lower Himalayas Genghis Khan saw in his path a marvellous-appearing animal, shaped like a deer, but green in colour and with only a single horn. He called Ye Liu Chutsai for an explanation of the phenomenon, and the Cathayan made answer gravely :

" This strange animal is called Kio-tuan. He knows every language of the earth, and he loves living men, and has a horror of slaying. His appearance is undoubtedly a warning to thee, O my Khan, to turn back from this path."

Under Ogotai, the son of Genghis Khan, the Cathayan practically administered the empire, and managed to take the infliction of punishment from the hands of Mongol officers, appointing magistrates to this duty, and tax-gatherers to the care of the treasures. His quick wit and quiet courage pleased the pagan conquerors, and he knew how to influence them. Ogotai was a heavy drinker, and Ye Liu Chutsai had reason to wish him to live as long as possible. Remonstrances having no effect upon the Khan, the Cathayan brought him an iron vase in which wine had been standing for some time. The wine had corroded the edge of the vessel.

" If wine," he said, " has eaten thus into iron, judge for yourself what it has done to your intestines."

Ogotai was struck by the demonstration and moderated his drinking—though it was the real cause of his death. Once, angered at an act of his councillor, he had Ye Liu Chutsai thrown into prison, but changed his mind later and ordered him to be freed. The Cathayan would not leave his cell Ogotai sent to find out why he did not appear at court.

"Thou didst name me thy minister," the sage sent back his response. "Thou hast placed me in prison. So, I was guilty. Thou hast set me at liberty. Thus, I am innocent. It is easy for thee to make game of me. But how am I to direct the affairs of the empire?"

He was restored to office, to the great good of millions of human beings. When Ogotai died the administration was taken out of the hands of the old Cathayan and given to a Mohammedan named Abd el Rahman. Grief over the oppressive measures of the new minister hastened the death of Chutsai.

Believing that he must have accumulated great riches during his life under the Khans, some Mongol officers searched his residence. They found no other treasure than a regular museum of musical instruments, manuscripts, maps, tablets and stones on which inscriptions had been carved.

XIII

OGOTAI AND HIS TREASURE

THE son who succeeded to the throne of the conqueror found himself an almost unwilling master of half the world. Ogotai had all a Mongol's good humour and tolerance, without the cruelty of his brothers. He could sit in his tent-palace at Kara-korum and do nothing except listen to the throngs who came to bow down at the throne of the Khan. His brothers and officers carried on the wars, and Ye Liu Chutsai saw to the gathering of the revenues.

Ogotai, broad of body and placid of mind, presents a curious picture—a benevolent barbarian with the spoils of Cathay, the women of a dozen empires and the horse herds of unlimited pastures—all at his summons. His actions are refreshingly unkinglike. When his officers protested at his habit of giving away whatever he happened to see, he replied that he would soon be gone out of the world and his only abiding place would be the memory of men.

He did not approve of the treasures amassed by the Persian and Indian monarchs. "They were fools," he said, "and it did them little good. They took nothing out of the world with them."

Shrewd Mohammedan merchants, hearing the rumour of his heedless generosity, did not fail to throng to his court with varied goods and a huge bill of account. Such bills were presented to the Khan every evening when he sat in public. Once the nobles in attendance protested to him that the merchants were overcharging him ridiculously. Ogotai assented.

"They came expecting to profit from me, and I do not wish them to go away disappointed."

His goings-abroad were something in the nature of a desert Haroun al Rashid's. He liked to talk with chance-met wanderers and on one occasion was struck by the poverty of an old man, who gave him three melons. Having no silver or rich cloth about him at the time, the Khan ordered one of his wives to reward the beggar with the pearls from her ear-rings which were of great size and value.

"It would be better, O my lord," she protested, "to summon him to court to-morrow and give him silver which he can put to more use than these pearls."

"The very poor," retorted the practical Mongol, "can not wait until the morrow. Besides, the pearls will come back to my treasury before long."

Ogotai had all a Mongol's fondness for hunting, and watching wrestling matches and horse races. Minstrels and athletes journeyed to his court from far Cathay and the cities of Persia. In his day began the feuds that eventually divided the Mongol dynasties —the strife between Mohammedan and Buddhist, between Persian and Chinese. This bickering annoyed the son of Genghis Khan. And his simplicity of mind sometimes discomfited the intriguers. A certain Buddhist came to the Mongol with a story that Genghis Khan had appeared before him in a dream, and had voiced a command.

"Go thou and bid my son exterminate all believers in Mohammed, for they are an evil race."

The severity of the dead conqueror toward the peoples of Islam was well known, and a *yarligh*—a command of the great Khan—delivered in a vision was an important matter. Ogotai meditated for a while.

"Did Genghis Khan address thee by the words of an interpreter?" he asked at length.

"Nay, O my Khan, he himself spoke."

"And thou knowest the Mongol speech?" persisted Ogotai.

It was an evident fact that the man honoured by the vision spoke nothing but Turki.

"Then thou hast lied to me," retorted the Khan, "for Genghis Khan spoke only Mongol." And he ordered the antagonist of the Mohammedans to be put to death.

Another time, some Chinese showmen were entertaining Ogotai with a puppet play. Among the marionettes, the Khan noticed a figure of an old man, turbaned, with long white moustaches, which was dragged about at the tail of a horse. He demanded that the Chinese explain the meaning of this.

"It is thus," responded the masters of the show, "that Mongol warriors draw after them Moslem captives."

Ogotai ordered the show to be stopped and his attendants to bring from his treasury the richest cloths, rugs and precious work both of China and Persia. He showed the Chinese that their goods were inferior to the western articles, and he added, "In my dominion there is no single rich Mohammedan who does not own several Chinese slaves—and no wealthy Chinese* has any Mohammedan slaves. You are aware, besides, that Genghis Khan gave command that a reward of forty pieces of gold should be given to the slayer of a Mohammedan, while he did not think the life of a Chinese worth a donkey. How, then, dare you mock the Mohammedans?" And he sent the showmen from the court with their marionettes.

---

* " On the heels of the military conqueror came the administrative mandarin "—L on Cahun " L'esprit bureaucratique des Chinois qui dirigaient l administration Mongole "—Blochet

The early Mongols never accustomed themselves to the use of money, and they had only contempt for the man who spent his life in hoarding it. Longfellow has put into verse the episode of the unfortunate kalif of Baghdad, who was overcome and captured in spite of a vast accumulation of treasury by Hulagu- Ogotai s celebrated nephew.

" I said to the Kalif, ' Thou art old ;
Thou hast no need of so much gold
Thou should st not have heaped and hidden it here
Till the breath of battle was hot and near "—

(For additional details on the lives of Ye Liu Chutsai and Ogotai, see the *Nouveaux Mélanges Asiatiques* of Abel-Rémusat, *Tartarie* by Louis Dubeux, *The Book of the Yuin*, translated from the Chinese annals by Father Amiot, and *Le Siècle des Youen* by M. Bazin.)

XIV

Being the Arrival of Fra Rubruquis at the Lashgar, or Travelling Court of Mangu Khan, the Grandson of Genghis Khan.

ONLY two Europeans have left us a description of the Mongols before the residence of the Khans was changed to Cathay. One is the monk Carpini, and the other the burly Fra Rubruquis, who rode with a stout heart into Tatary, half convinced that he would be tortured to death. On behalf of his royal master, Saint Louis of France, he went not as an envoy of his king, but as an emissary of peace, in the hope that the pagan conquerors might be moved somewhat to refrain from warfare against Europe.

For fellowship he had only a badly frightened brother monk—Constantinople left behind them and the steppes of Asia closing around them. He had been chilled to the marrow and half starved, and jolted for three thousand miles. The Mongols had equipped him with sheepskins and felt foot-socks and boots and hoods of skin, and had been careful to select a powerful horse for him each day during the long journey from the Volga frontier, because he was corpulent and heavy.

He was a mystery to the Mongols—a long-robed

* As given in Astley's Voyages, but modified and condensed.

and barefoot man out of the far land of the Franks,
who was neither merchant nor ambassador, who
carried no arms, gave no presents and would accept
no reward. A curious picture, this, of the weighty
and dogmatic friar who had wandered out of stricken
Europe to behold the Khan—a poverty-ridden, but
not a humble member of the long train that journeyed
east into the desert—Yaroslav, duke of Russia,
Cathayan and Turkish lords, the sons of the king of
Georgia, the envoy of the kalif of Baghdad, and the
great sultans of the Saracens. And, with an observant
eye, Rubruquis has described for us the court of the
nomad conquerors, where the " barons " drank milk
in jewel encrusted goblets and rode in sheepskins
upon saddles ornamented with gold work.

In this fashion he describes his arrival at the court
of Mangu Khan :

On Saint Stephen's day in December we came to
a great plain where not a hillock was to be seen, and
the next day we arrived at the court of the great
Khan.

Our guide had a large house appointed for him,
and only a small cottage was given to us three—
hardly room enough for our baggage, beds and a
small fire. Many came to our guide with drink made
of rice in long-necked bottles, no different from the
best wine except that it smelt otherwise. We were
called out and questioned about our business. A secretary told me that we wanted the assistance of a Tartar
army against the Saracens ; and this astonished me
as I knew the letters from your majesty* required

* Saint Louis, King of France, who was then a captive of the Mamluks.

no army and only advised the Khan to be a friend to all Christians.

The Mongols then demanded if we would make peace with them. To this I answered, " Having done no wrong, the King of the French hath given no cause for war. If warred against without cause, we trust in the help of God."

At this they seemed all amazed, exclaiming, " Did you not come to make peace ? "

The day following I went to the court barefoot, at which the people stared ; but a Hungarian boy who was among them and knew our order,* told them the reason. Whereupon a Nestorian who was the chief secretary of the court asked many questions of us and we went back to our lodgings.

On the way, at the end of the court toward the east, I saw a small house with a little cross above it. At this I rejoiced, believing there might be some Christians within. I entered boldly, and found an altar well furnished, having a golden cloth adorned with images of Christ, the Virgin, Saint John the Baptist and two angels—the lines of their bodies and garments shaped with small pearls.

On the altar was a large silver cross, bright with precious stones and many embroiderings, Before it burned a lamp with eight lights. Sitting beside the altar I saw an Armenian monk somewhat black and lean, clad in a rough hairy coat and girded with iron under his haircloth.

Before saluting the monk, we fell flat on the ground, singing *Ave regina* and other hymns, and the monk

---

* Rubruquis was a Franciscan, and the first priest to appear in his robes in far Asia—Carpini, the envoy of the Pope, having put on secular dress.

joined in our prayers. We then sat down by the monk
who had a small fire in a pan before him. He told us
that he—a hermit of Jerusalem—had come a month
before us.

When we had talked for a while we went on to our
lodgings, making a little broth of flesh and millet for
our supper. Our Mongol guide and his companions
were very drunk at court and little care was taken of
us. So great was the cold that next morning the ends
of my toes were frost-bitten and I could no longer
go barefoot.

From the time when the frost begins, it never
ceases until May, and even then it freezes every night
and morning. And, while we were there, the cold,
rising with the wind, killed multitudes of animals.
The people of the court* brought us ram-skin coats
and breeches and shoes, which my companion and the
interpreter accepted. On the fifth of January we
were taken into the court.

It was asked of us what reverence we would pay
the Khan, and I said that we came from a far country
and with their leave would first sing praises to God
who had brought us hither in safety, and would afterwards do whatever might please the Khan. Then
they went into the presence and related what we had
told them. Returning, they brought us before the
entrance of the hall, lifting up the felt which hung
before the threshold, and we sang *A solis ortus cardine.*
They searched the breasts of our robes to see if

* When Rubruquis speaks of the court, he means the quarters of Mangu
Khan, his women and higher officers, in the centre of the encampment.
Of the encampment of Batu—Mangu's cousin—on the Volga, he says, " We
were astonished at the magnificence of his encampment   The houses and
tents stretched out to a vast length, and there were great numbers of people
ranged round for three or four leagues."

we had any weapons concealed, and they made our interpreter leave his girdle and knife with one of the guards at the door. When we entered, our interpreter was made to stand at a table which was well furnished with mare's milk, and we were placed on a bench before the women.

The whole house was hung with cloth-of-gold, and on the hearth in the middle there was a fire of thorns, worm-wood roots and cow-dung. The Khan sat upon a couch covered with bright and shining fur like seal's skin. He was a flat-nosed man of middle stature, about forty-five years of age, and one of his wives—a pretty little woman—sat beside him. Likewise one of his daughters, a hard-favoured young woman, sat on a couch near him. This house had belonged to the mother of this daughter, who was a Christian, and the daughter was now mistress of it.

We were asked whether we would drink rice-wine, or mare's milk or mead made of honey—for they use these three kinds of liquors in winter. I answered that we had no pleasure in drink and would be content with what the Khan pleased to order. So we were served with rice-wine, of which I tasted a little out of respect.

After a long interval during which the Khan amused himself with falcons and other birds, we were commanded to speak and had to bow the knee. The Khan had his interpreter, a Nestorian, but our interpreter had been given so much liquor from the table that he was quite drunk. I addressed the Khan as follows :

" We give thanks and praise to God who hath brought us from such remote parts of the world to

the presence of Mangu Khan on whom he hath bestowed
such great power. The Christians of the west, especially
the King of the French, sent us unto him with letters,
entreating him to allow us to stay in his country, as it
is our office to teach men the law of God. We therefore beg his highness to permit us to remain. We have
neither silver nor gold nor precious stones to offer,
but we present ourselves to do service."

The Khan answered to this effect :

" Even as the sun sheds his beams everywhere, so
our power and that of Batu extends everywhere, so
we have no need of your gold or silver."

I entreated his highness not to be displeased with me
for mentioning gold and silver, as I spoke only to
make clear our desire to do him service. Hitherto
I had understood our interpreter, but he was now drunk
and could not utter an intelligible sentence and it
appeared to me that the Khan might be drunk likewise ; wherefore I held my peace.

Then he made us rise and sit down again, and after
a few words of compliment we withdrew from the
presence. One of the secretaries and interpreters went
out with us and was very inquisitive about the kingdom of France, particularly whether it had plenty of
sheep, cattle, and horses, as if they meant to make it
all their own. They appointed one to take care of us
and we went to the Armenian monk, whither came
the interpreter, saying that Mangu Khan gave
us two months to stay, until the extreme cold be
past.

To this I answered, " God preserve Mangu Khan
and grant him a long life. We have found this monk
whom we think a holy man and we will willingly

R

remain and pray with him for the well-being of the Khan."

(For on feast days the Christians come to court and pray for him and bless his cup, after which the Saracen priests do the same and after them the idolatrous priests.* The monk Sergius pretended that he only believed the Christians, but in this Sergius lied. The Khan believes none, but all follow his court as flies do honey. He gives to all, and all think they are his familiars, and all prophesy prosperity to him.)

We then went to our dwelling which we found very cold as we had no fuel and were still fasting—though by then it was night. But he who had the care of us provided us with some wood and a little food, and our guide of the journey hither, who was now to return to Batu, begged a carpet from us. This we gave him and he departed in peace.

The cold became severe, and Mangu Khan sent us three fur coats with the hair outward, which we took gratefully. But we explained that we had not fit quarters to pray for the Khan—our cottage being so small we could scarcely stand up in it, neither could we open our books after lighting the fire, on account of the smoke. The Khan sent to ask the monk if he would be pleased with our company, who gladly received us and after this we had a better house.

While we were absent, Mangu Khan himself came into the chapel and a golden bed was fetched, upon which he sat with his queen opposite the altar. We were then sent for and a pavilion guard searched us for hidden weapons. On going in with a Bible and a breviary in my bosom, I first bowed down before the

* Buddhists, with whom Rubruquis had no previous acquaintance.

altar and then made obeisance to Mangu Khan, who caused our books to be brought to him and asked the meaning of the miniatures with which they were adorned. The Nestorians answered him as they thought proper, because we had not our interpreter. Being desired to sing a psalm after our manner, we chanted *Veni, Sanctu Spiritus*. Then the Khan left, but the lady remained and distributed gifts.

I honoured the monk Sergius as my bishop. In many things he acted in a way that much displeased me, for he had made for himself a cap of peacock feathers, with a small gold cross. But I was well pleased with the cross. The monk by my suggestion craved leave to carry the cross aloft on a lance, and Mangu gave permission to carry it in any way we saw fit.

So we went about with Sergius, for the honour of the cross, as he had fashioned a banner on a cane as long as a lance, and we carried it throughout the tents of the Tatars, singing *Vexilla regis prodcunt*, to the great regret of the Mohammedans, who were envious of our favour, and of the Nestorian priests, who were envious of the profit he had from its use.

Near Karakorum, Mangu has a large court, surrounded by a brick wall, like our priories. Within that court is a great palace where the Khan holds feasts twice in the year, in Easter and in summer, when he displays all his magnificence. Because it was indecent to have flagons going about the hall of the palace as in a tavern, William Bouchier, the goldsmith from Paris, built a great silver tree just without the middle entrance of the hall. At the roots of the tree were four silver lions from which flowed pure cow's milk.

On the four great boughs of the tree were twined golden serpents that discharge streams of wine of various sorts.

The palace is like a church with three aisles and two rows of pillars. The Khan sits on a high place at the north wall, where he may be seen of all. The space between the Khan and the silver tree is left vacant for the coming and the going of the cup-bearers and the messengers who bring gifts. On the right side of the Khan the men sit and on the left the women. Only one woman sits beside him, not so high as he.

Except for the palace of the Khan, Karakorum is not so fine as the town of Saint Denis. It has two main streets, that of the Saracens where the fairs are held, and the street of the Cathayans which is filled with craftsmen. Besides, there are many palaces in which are the courts of the secretaries of the Khan— also markets for millet and grain, sheep and horses and oxen and wagons. There are twelve idol temples, two Mohammedan mosques and one Nestorian church.

About Passion Sunday the Khan departed for Karakorum, with his smaller houses* only, and the monk and we followed. On the journey we had to pass through hilly country, where we encountered high winds, extreme cold and much snow. About midnight the Khan sent to the monk and us, requesting us to pray to God to make the storm cease as the animals of his train were like to die, being mostly with young. The monk sent him incense, desiring him to put it on the coals as an offering. Whether he

---

* *Kibitkas*, or wagon tents.

did this or no, I know not, but the wind and snow ceased, which had lasted two days.

On Palm Sunday we were near Karakorum and at dawn of day we blessed the willow boughs on which there were as yet no buds. About nine o'clock we entered the city, carrying the cross aloft and passing through the street of the Saracens. We proceeded to the church where the Nestorians met us in procession. After Mass, it being now evening, William Bouchier the goldsmith brought us to sup at his lodging. He had a wife born in Hungary, and we found here also Basilicus, the son of an Englishman.

After supper we retired to our cottage which, like the oratory of the monk, was near the Nestorian church—a church of size very handsomely built, the ceiling covered with silk embroidered with gold.

We remained in the city to celebrate the festival of Easter. There was a vast multitude of Hungarians, Alans, Ruthenians or Russians and Georgians and Armenians, who had not received the sacrament since they were taken prisoners. The Nestorians entreated me to celebrate the festival, and I had neither vestments nor altar.

But the goldsmith furnished me with vestments, and made an oratory on a chariot, decently painted with Scripture histories; he made also a silver box and an image of the blessed Virgin.

Until now I had hoped for the arrival of the king of Armenia, and a certain German priest who was likewise expected. Hearing nothing of the king and fearing the severity of another winter, I sent to ask the pleasure of the Khan, whether we were to remain or to leave him.

Next day some of the chief secretaries of the Khan came to me, one a Mongol who is cup-bearer to the Khan, and the rest Saracens. These men demanded on behalf of the Khan wherefore I had come to them? To this I answered that Batu had ordered me to the Khan, to whom I had nothing to say on behalf of any man, unless I were to repeat the words of God, if he would hear them.

Then they demanded what words I would speak, thinking I meant to prophesy prosperous things as others had done.

I therefore said : " To Mangu I would say that God hath given much, for the power and riches that he enjoys come not from the idols of the Buddhists."

Then they asked if I had been in Heaven, that I should know the commandments of God? And they went to Mangu saying that I had said he was an idolater and a Buddhist, who kept not the commandments of God. On the morrow the Khan sent again, explaining that he knew we had no message for him, but came to pray for him as other priests did, yet he wished to know if any of our ambassadors had ever been in his country. Then I declared unto them all I knew respecting David and Friar Andrew, all of which was put down in writing and laid before Mangu.

On Whitsunday I was called into the presence of the Khan. Before I went in, the goldsmith's son who was now my interpreter informed me that the Mongols had determined I was to return to my own country, and advised me to say nothing against it.

When I came before the Khan I kneeled, and he asked me whether I had said to his secretaries that he was a Buddhist. To this I answered, "My lord, I said not so."

"I thought well you said not so," he answered, "for it was a word you ought not to have spoken." Then, reaching forth the staff on which he leaned toward me, he said, "Be not afraid."

To this I answered, smiling, that if I had feared I should not have come hither.

"We Mongols believe there is but one God," he said then, "and we have an upright heart toward him."

"Then," I responded, "may God grant you this mind, for without His gift it cannot be."

"God hath given to the hand divers fingers," he added, "and hath given many ways to man. He hath given the Scriptures to you, yet you keep them not. Surely it is not in your Scriptures that one of you should dispraise another."

"Nay," said I, "and I signified to your highness from the beginning that I would not contend with any one."

"I speak not," said he, "of you. In like manner, it is not in your Scriptures that a man should turn from justice for the sake of profit."

To this I answered that I had not come to seek money, having even refused what was offered me. And one of the secretaries then present avowed that I had refused a bar of silver and a piece of silk.

"I speak not of that," said the Khan. "God hath given to you the Scriptures and ye keep them not ; but he hath given to us soothsayers, and we do what they bid us and live in peace."

He drank four times, I think, before uttering this,

and, while I waited attentively in expectation that he might disclose more respecting his faith, he spoke again :

"You have stayed a long time here and it is my pleasure that you return. You have said that you dared not take my ambassador with you. Will you take, then, my messenger or my letters ? "

To this I answered, if the Khan would make me understand his words and put them in writing, I would willingly carry them to the best of my power.

He then asked if I would have gold or silver or costly garments, and I answered that we were accustomed to accept no such things, yet could not get out of his country without his help. He explained that he would provide for us, and demanded how far we wished to be taken. I said it were sufficient if he had us conveyed to Armenia.

"I will cause you to be carried thither," he made answer, "after which, look to yourself. There are two eyes in a single head, yet they both behold one object. You came from Batu, and therefore you must return to him."

Then, after a pause, as if musing, he said, "You have a long way to go. Make yourself strong with food, that you may be able to endure the journey."

So he ordered them to give me drink, and I departed from his presence and returned not again.

XV

A LITTLE-KNOWN chapter of history is the contact of the Mongols with the Armenians and the Christians of Palestine after the death of Genghis Khan. Hulagu, his grandson, brother of Mangu who was then Khan, took over the dominion of Persia, Mesopotamia and Syria in the middle of the thirteenth century. What followed is well summarised in the *Cambridge Medieval History*, Vol. IV, p. 175.

"After more than a century's experience the Armenians could not trust their Latin* neighbours as allies. Haithon (king of the Armenians) put his trust not in the Christians but in the heathen Mongols who for half a century were to prove the best friends Armenia ever had.

"At the beginning of Haithon's reign the Mongols . . . did good service to the Armenians by conquering the Seljuks. Haithon made an offensive and defensive alliance with Baichu the Mongol general† and in 1244 became the vassal of the Khan Ogotai. Ten years later, he did homage in person to Mangu

* The crusading barons who still maintained their fiefs in the Holy Land, notably Bohemond of Antioch
† Bachu in the text, as also Hethum, Ogdai, etc The spelling has been altered to conform with the other chapters of this book Baichu is often confused with Batu, who was a grandson of Genghis Khan, and the first ruler of the Golden Horde in Russia.

Khan and cemented the friendship between the two nations by a long stay at the Mongol court.

"The rest of his reign was filled with a struggle against the Mamluks, whose northward advance was fortunately opposed by the Mongols. Haithon and Hulagu joined forces at Edessa to undertake the capture of Jerusalem from the Mamluks."

Bibliography

I

SOURCES

THE earliest source was the Mongolian *Altyn debter*, the Golden Book, now lost. Upon this was based the Chinese *Yuan shi* or Mongol Annals, and the history of Rashid ed-Din. (See below.)

Another Mongolian work called the Secret History is preserved only in the Chinese translation, the *Yuan ch'ao mi shi*, originally written (1228) in Mongol, in Ugur letters by a contemporary of the great Khan.

In the mid-seventeenth century the best known of the Mongol annalists, Ssanang Setzen, compiled his *Chung taishi* (*Khadun Toghudji*), a legendary account of the ancestors and life of Genghis Khan. It is distorted with Buddhist myths, but gives us the only intimate picture of the early Mongols. Translated into Russian by the Archimandrite Hyacinth, and thence—at least in part—into German by Isaac Jacob Schmidt in 1829. (See below.)

Of the Chinese sources, the most important are:

The *T'oung kien kang mou*, or history of the imperial dynasties, compiled by Ssi ma Kouang. This has very little to say about the early Mongol rulers. Available in a French translation of doubtful value, to-day, the *Histoire générale de la Chine, traduite du*

Tong-Kien-Kang-Mou par le Père Joseph-Anne-Marie de Moyriac de Mailla, dirigée par M. le Roux des Hautesrayes, Paris, 1777-1778.

The *Ch'in chêng lu,* by an anonymous writer, gives a narrative of the Mongols beginning with Yesukai and ending with the death of Ogotai.

From this, and the *Yuan ch'ao mi shi,* the most important of the Chinese sources, the *Yuan Shi,* or Mongol Annals, was compiled in 1370. It is more accurate than the work of Ssanang Setzen, but—as in the case of the Mongol sagas—of doubtful value when it deals with the western countries. It has been translated into French under the title of the *Histoire de Gentchiscan et de toute la dinastie des Mongous, tirée de l'Histoire Chinoise* by Anthony Gaubil, Paris, 1739.

By all odds the most valuable source is the *Jami-ut-Tavarikh,* or Collection of Annals, by Fadl'allah Rashid ed-Din, a Persian who was administrator of Persia under Ghazan Khan in the late thirteenth century. "There remain," said Rashid in his introduction, "in the archives of the Mongol Khan of Persia some historical fragments of acknowledged authority written in the Mongol language and characters." . . . In his task of translating and clarifying these documents Rashid—a most gifted historian—was aided by a staff of historians, Chinese Ugurs and Turks, and by the Mongols themselves. Unfortunately, the *Jami-ut-Tavarikh* is still untranslated, but has been published by Vrosset in the Gibbs Memorial Series, Leyden and London.

The *Tarikh-i-Jahan Gushai,* or History of the World Conqueror, by Ala ed-Din Ata Malik, called Juvaini, written in 1257 or 1260 (Gibbs Memorial

Series, London, 1912-14), is almost of equal value, but disappointing to the biographer of Genghis Khan in that it gives at first hand only an account of the last ten years of the reign of the conqueror.

Another contemporary source is the *K'amil-ut-Tavarikh* of Ibn Athir, called Nissavi, 1231. This is rather the history of Jelal ed-Din and the Persian wars.

The later works of Khwándamír, the *Habiba Siyar*, 1523, and the *Raudata Safa*, 1470, of his grandfather, Mírkhwánd, contain only fragmentary notices of Genghis Khan. So also does the *Fateh Nameh Tavarikh al Osman*, or Osman History of Abulcaïr, 1550.

II

HISTORIES OF GENGHIS KHAN AND THE EARLY MONGOLS FROM THE SOURCES*

ABU AL FARAJ, GREGORIUS. (Bar Hebreaus.) *Historia Dynastiorium.*

> (The Syrian Gregorius lived in the mid-thirteenth century, and came into contact with the Mongols. His history of dynasties is valuable, and his anecdotes are unique. Translated into Latin by Pocock, 1663.)

ABULGHAZI BAHADUR KHAN. *Histoire généalogique des Tartars*, Leyden, 1726.

> (The author, an Uzbek khan, wrote in the seventeenth century, drawing most of his information from Rashid. Interesting, but of little value to the student until the author deals with his own period.)

---

* Most of the sources for the life of Genghis Khan exist only in manuscript form, untranslated. The volumes in Group II are rare for the most part. Books that may be found in the larger public libraries and university libraries are marked with an asterisk.

Douglas, Robert Kennaway. The Life of Jenghiz Khan translated from the Chinese, London, 1877.
> (Summarized in the Encyclopædia Britannica.)

Erdmann, Franz von. *Vollstaendige Uebersicht der aeltesten tuerkischen, tatarischen und mogholischen Voelkerstaemme nach Raschid-ud-Din's Vorgânge,* Kazan, 1841.
Temudschin der Unerschütterliche, Leipzig, 1862.

Krause, F. E. A. *Cingis Han. Die Geschichte seines lebens nach der Chinesischen Reichsannalen,* Heidelberg, 1922.
> (A short account of the Khan from the Chinese annals.)

Geschichte Ostasiens, Göttengen, 1925.
> (An excellent summary of the Mongol conquests.)

Petis de la Croix. *Histoire du Grand Genghizcan Premier Empereur des Anciens Mogols traduite de plusieurs Auteurs Orientaux & de Voyageurs Européens,* Paris, 1710.
> (The author devoted ten years to a translation of the Persian and Arabic sources. He did not consult the Chinese annals and the chief interest of his work to-day is in its details and anecdotes of the Persian campaign.)

Schmidt, Isaac Jacob. *Geschichte der Ost-Mongolen, etc., verfasst von Ssanang Setzen Chung-taidshi,* St. Petersburg, 1829.
> (A valuable translation from the Mongol saga, unfortunately excessively rare.)

Vladimirtzov, B. J. *Jenghis Khan,* Berlin and Moscow, 1922.
> (A work of 176 pp. in Russian that refers frequently to the " Yuen-cao-mi-si.")

III

GENERAL HISTORIES OF THE MONGOLS

BARTHOLD, WILHELM. *Turkestan im Zeitalter des Mongoleneinfalls,* St. Petersburg, 1900.

(Devoted in large part to Genghis Khan, and con taining matter from the sources not hitherto published elsewhere.)

Die Entstehung des Reiches Tchinghiz-chans, St. Petersburg, 1896.

CAHUN, LEON. *Introduction à l'histoire de l'Asie : Turcs et Mongols, des origines à* 1405, Paris, 1896.

(A curiously valuable book. The author, a brilliant linguist, drew material from many sources, but became fascinated by Turkish legends and Mongol military achievement.)

*CORDIER, HENRI. *Histoire Générale de la Chine et de ses relations avec les pays étrangers,* Paris, 1920.

(Notable for its account of the contact of China with the west. The sketch of Genghis Khan in Vol. II . is drawn chiefly from de Mailla and d'Ohsson.)

*CURTIN, JEREMIAH. *The Mongols,* Boston, 1908.

(A popular translation of the Mongol sagas, it is uncertain from what source.)

DE GUIGNES, J. *Histoire générale des Huns, des Turcs, des Mogols,* Paris, 1756.

(A gigantic work, from Chinese and other sources. It has little value to-day.)

Howorth, Sir Henry H. *History of the Mongols*, London, 1876-88.

(A monumental work, valuable to the student, based mainly upon Erdmann and d'Ohsson.)

Mouradga d'Ohsson. *Histoire des Mongols depuis Tchinguiz-Khan jusqu'à Timour Bey*, The Hague and Amsterdam, 1834-5.

(A full and informative history of the Mongols, from the Persian and Arab writers—though Gaubil has also been consulted. Like M. Cordier, Baron d'Ohsson is antagonistic to Genghis Khan, and reveals him only as a military commander of the Mongols.)

IV

ACCOUNTS OF THE EARLY VOYAGERS

Bergeron, Pierre. *Relation des voyages en Tartarie de Fr. Gvillavme de Rvbrvqvis, Fr. Jean dv Plan Carpin. Plvs vn traicté des Tartares*, Paris, 1634.

(The treatise on the "Tartars" is remarkable for its day.)

*Carpini, John of Plano. Hakluyt Society, London, 1900, II Series, Vol. IV.

(The first European to visit the Mongols, less than a generation after the death of Genghis Khan.)

Ibn Batuta. Translated by Défrémery and Sanguinetti, Paris, 1853.

(The travels of the celebrated Arab who passed through most of Asia at the end of the Mongol dominion.)

*MARCO POLO. The Book of Marco Polo, translated by Sir Henry Yule and edited by Henri Cordier, London, 1921.

*RUBRUQUIS (WILLIAM OF RUBRUK). The Journey of William of Rubruk to the eastern parts of the World, Hakluyt Society, London, 1900. II Series, Vol. IV.

V

MISCELLANEOUS

BAZIN, M. *Le Siècle des Youên, ou tableau historique de la littérature Chinoise depuis l'avénement des empereurs mongols*, Paris, 1850.

*BRETSCHNEIDER, E. *Medieval Researches from Eastern Asiatic Sources*, London, 1888.

(Bits of the geography of Ye Liu Chutsai and a summary of the western campaigns of Genghis Khan.)

*BROWNE, EDWARD GRANVILLE. *A Literary History of Persia*. Vol. II from Firdawsi to Sa'di. Vol. III under Tartar Dominion. Cambridge, 1906-1920.

(Contains a good modern dissertation on the Mongols.)

Cambridge Medieval History, Vol. IV, the Eastern Roman Empire, New York, 1923.

(A summary of the Mongol conquests, with a new appreciation of their importance.)

CORDIER, HENRI. *Mélanges d'Histoire et de Géographie Orientales*, Tome II, Paris, 1920.

(The Mongol invasion of Europe.)

DUBEUX, LOUIS. *Tartarie*, Paris, 1840.

DULAURIER, EDOUARD. *Les Mongols d'après les historiens arméniens.* *Journal Asiatique*, 5th ser., 1858, pp. 192-255. Also 1860, pp. 295-306.

FEER, LEON. *La Puissance et la Civilisation Mongoles au treizieme siècle*, Paris, 1867.

JOINVILLE. (Edited by Francisque-Michel) Paris, 1867.
(One of the best of the medieval chronicles.)

JORDAIN, CATALANI P. *Mirabilia Descripta sequitur de Magno Tartaro.*
(A medieval viewpoint. To this might be added the Relations taken out of Roger Wendover and Matthew Paris, in Purchas.)

JULG, BERNHARD. On the Present State of Mongolian Researches, J.R.A.S., January, 1882.

*LANE-POOLE, STANLEY. The Mohammedan Dynasties, Westminster, 1894.

MONTGOMERY, JAMES A. *The History of Yaballaha III.* New York, 1927.
(A translation of the Syriac chronicle of the journey of the Mongol bishop to Rome late in the thirteenth century.)

WERNER, E. T. C. *The Burial Place of Genghis Khan.* Journal of the North China Branch of the Royal Asiatic Society. Vol. LVI—1925.

MOSHEIM, J. L. *Historia Tartarorum ecclesiastica*, Helmstadt, 1741.

*Parker, E. H. *A Thousand Years of the Tatars*, New York, 1924.

(An excellent account of the Tatar peoples up to the birth of Genghis Khan.)

Petis de la Croix, Francois (the son of de la Croix, the author of the life of Genghis Khan). *Abrégé Chronologique de l'Histoire Ottomane*, Paris, 1768.

(Summaries of the rulers of the Mongol peoples from Genghis Khan to the seventeenth century.)

Quatremere, M. *Histoire des Mongols de la Perse par Raschid-eldin, traduite, accompagnée de notes*, Paris, 1836.

(The life of Rashid, and the splendid notes on Mongol customs would make this valuable, even if it were not the only translation of Rashid, though merely a portion of the *Jami-ut-Tavarikh*.)

Rémusat, Jean Pierre Abel. *Nouveaux Mélanges Asiatiques*, Paris, 1829.

(Sketches of Subotai, Ye Liu Chutsai and others.)

Observations sur l'Histoire des Mongols orientaux de Ssanang Setzen, Paris, 1832.

Rémusat, Jean Pierre Abel. *Mémoires sur les relations politiques des princes Chrétiens et parculièrement des Rois de France avec les Empereurs Mongols.*

Institut Royal, Mémoires de l'Académie des inscriptions et belles lettres. Paris, 1822.

(An important summary of the correspondence between the Mongols and the monarchs of Europe, well worth reading.)

Mélanges posthumes et de littérature Orientales—Analyse de l'histoire des Mongols de Sanang-Setsen. Paris, 1843.

*STUBE, RUDOLF. *Tschingizchan: seine Staatsbildung und seine Persöhnlichkeit.* In *Neue Jahrbücher für das klassische Altertum,* Vol. XXI, 1908, pp. 532-541.
> (A brief commentary on the conqueror.)

TIMKOWSKI, IGOR FEDOROVICH. Travels of the Russian Mission through Mongolia to China. With Corrections and Notes by Klaproth, London, 1827.
> (Translated apparently from the French. Valuable geographic and historical research by a member of one of the Russian embassies.)

VISDELOU, CLAUDE. Supplement to D'Herbelot's *Bibliothèque Orientale*, Paris, 1780.

*YULE, SIR HENRY. *Cathay and the Way Thither,* Revised by Cordier Hakluyt Society, 2nd series, Nos. 33, 37, 38, 41.

Index

A

B

277

Printed at the BURLEIGH PRESS, *Lewin's Mead*, BRISTOL.

CPSIA information can be obtained
at www.ICGtesting.com
Printed in the USA
LVHW051149010221
677997LV00002B/93

9 781296 501075